Big Mamma's
ITALIAN-AMERICAN
Cookbook

LEE CASAZZA
**** ****
COOKING

Teresa Lapetina
"Big Mamma"
1940

Big Mamma's
ITALIAN-AMERICAN
Cookbook

LEE CASAZZA

Easy and Delicious Favorites from Our Family

www.leecasazzacooking.com

Cover, book design, and drawings by Robert Paul Casazza
Photographs by Lee Casazza
Photography consulting by Brandon Paul Casazza
Editor & Final Proofreader: Lisa Gordanier, Hidden Hand Editing

Publisher's Cataloging-In-Publication Data
(Prepared by The Donohue Group, Inc.)

Casazza, Lee.
Big Mamma's Italian-American cookbook / Lee Casazza. -- First edition.

pages : color illustrations ; cm

"Easy and delicious favorites from our family."
Includes index.
ISBN: 978-0-615-96286-3

1. Cooking, Italian. 2. Cooking, American. 3. Cookbooks. I. Title.

TX723 .C39 2014
641.5945   2014911500

Library of Congress Control Number: 2014911500

Published by Lee Casazza Cooking, LLC

Cover image: Rustic Pizza with Roasted Grapes, Prosciutto & Arugula, page 52

Printed and bound in the
United States of America

10 9 8 7 6 5 4 3 2 1

For Bob, Brandon, Angie, Dotti,
all Italian-Americans, and
Italian-Canadians

Contents

Our Family

Teresa Lapetina & Vincenzio Greco

1881 – 1970   1877 – 1953

Teresa Lapetina and Vincenzio Greco sailed to America on the *Spartan Prince* from Naples, Italy on the 23rd of July, 1898. They were from the small town of Picerno, in the province of Potenza, in the southern region of Basilicata. On the passenger manifest, his occupation was shown as "shoemaker" and she called herself a "country woman." They lived New York City, Reading, Pennsylvania, and Portsmouth, Virginia.

Ernesto Noviello & Elisabetta Greco

1895 – 1980   1899 – 1992

Ernesto Noviello was from the small village of Montefalcione, Avellino, in the Campania region of Italy. In 1913, he sailed from Naples to start a new life in America. Elisabetta Greco was born in Little Italy, New York City. Her family later moved to Portsmouth, Virginia, where she and Ernesto met. After they were married, he "Americanized" the family name to Novello.

Paolo Casazza & Rose Biggio

1889 – 1973   1893 – 1931

In 1870, the first Casazzas made the crossing to New York. Paolo (Paul) Casazza was born in Manhattan to immigrant parents. Rose was also born in Manhattan to immigrant parents. They were married in 1912 and settled in Brooklyn, New York. Rose died at age 37 from strep throat, sadly a decade before penicillin was available to the public. Paul and his two sisters raised his five children.

Theodore R. Casazza & Marie Noviello

1920 – 1994   1923 – 2005

Marie was born in Portsmouth, Virginia. Ted grew up in Bay Ridge, Brooklyn, New York with two brothers and two sisters. In 1940, he enlisted in the Marines. His first station was Norfolk, Virginia. One evening, Ted and a Naval lieutenant visited the Noviello home in Richmond, Virginia, where he met Marie. They were married in December of 1942, but Ted spent most of the next two years serving in the Pacific aboard the U.S.S. *Montpelier*.

Appetizers

"Antipasti"

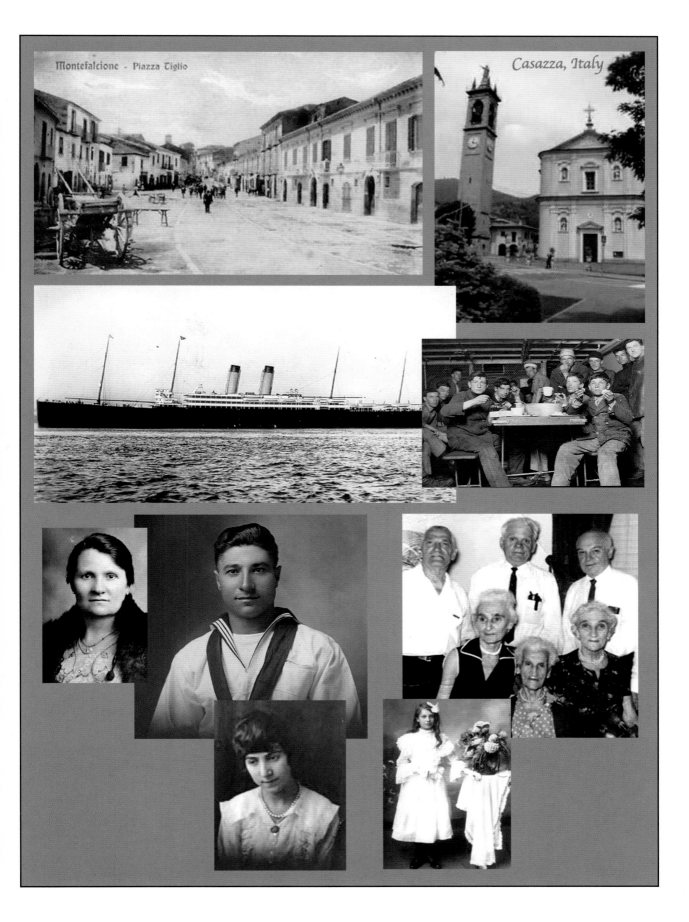

Montefalcione - Piazza Tiglio

Casazza, Italy

Bruschette di Pomodori

The aromas of ripe tomatoes and fresh basil fill the kitchen, and it makes me feel like I am in Positano . . . in the summer. Bruschetta (singular) comes from the Latin word *bruscare,* which means to toast or burn. Most people pronounce this incorrectly. You should pronounce it "Bru-SKEH-tah," as if it were spelled with the letter "K," not using the sound of "CH." Bruschette (plural) is pronounced "Bru-SKEH-tay."

2 cups (500 ml) diced cherry tomatoes or other ripe tomatoes
1 clove garlic, minced
¼ cup (60 ml) extra-virgin olive oil
¼ cup (60 ml) chopped fresh basil
Salt and freshly ground black pepper
1 French baguette, cut into ½-inch (12-mm) slices

Place all of the ingredients except the bread in a medium bowl. Stir lightly and set aside for 30 minutes. Place the bread slices on a baking sheet and bake in a 400 F (200 C) degree oven until golden brown on both sides. Let cool. Spoon a little juice from the tomatoes on each of the bread slices and then spoon on the tomatoes.

Bruschette are sliced thicker, baked in the oven until golden or grilled on a grill pan, sometimes rubbed with a cut piece of garlic, and topped with cold or room-temperature ingredients.

Crostini are sliced thinner, brushed with olive oil, baked in the oven or grilled on a grill pan until golden, and spread with room-temperature or warm ingredients.

Bruschette di Prosciutto

This appetizer is so easy to prepare, but you must use Prosciutto di Parma. It costs more but you only need a small amount to serve as an appetizer for four people. Serve along with a bowl of Italian olives.

1 French baguette, cut into ½-inch (12-mm) slices
Extra-virgin olive oil
2 large cloves garlic, cut in half lengthwise
¼ lb (125 g) Prosciutto di Parma, thinly sliced
3 very ripe Roma tomatoes, cut in half lengthwise

Bake bread slices in a 400 F (200 C) degree oven until golden brown on both sides.
Rub one side of each slice of bread with garlic, then rub with the tomato slices to get the juice all over the top side of the bread.
Drizzle with a little of the extra-virgin olive oil and top with a slice of prosciutto; drizzle again with olive oil.

Crostini with Black Olives & Fennel

Crostini con Olive Nere e Finocchio

There is something wonderful about the combination of sautéed olives and fennel.

1 French baguette, cut into ¼-inch (6-mm) slices
1 medium bulb fennel, fronds removed (save some for garnish), diced
2 T (30 ml) extra-light olive oil or grape seed oil
¼ medium onion, diced
1 clove garlic, minced
½ t (2 ml) red pepper flakes
Salt and freshly ground black pepper
1 cup (250 ml) pitted and chopped Italian black olives

Grill bread slices on a grill pan over medium-high heat until golden brown on both sides.
In a skillet over low heat, sauté the fennel in the oil for 10 minutes.
Add the onion and continue to sauté for another 10 minutes.
Add the garlic and red pepper flakes, and season to taste with salt and pepper.
Sauté another couple of minutes; add the black olives and heat through.
Spoon the olive-fennel mixture on top of each slice of bread and top with some fennel fronds.

Roasted Eggplant Spread
Crema di Melanzane

This is a very healthy antipasto spread for bruschette or crostini. It is also a delicious spread with carrots or celery for a light lunch or snack. It's perfect for picnics because it is served at room temperature. If you don't have pine nuts (pignoli), substitute walnuts.

2 medium eggplants,
  peeled and chopped
2 red bell peppers,
  seeded and chopped
½ large sweet onion, diced
4 cloves garlic, cut in half
3 T (45 ml) extra-light olive oil
  or grape seed oil
½ t (2 ml) red pepper flakes
Salt and freshly ground black pepper
½ cup (125 ml) pine nuts or walnuts
Zest and juice of 1 lemon
5 to 6 large basil leaves
1 (14 oz/398 ml) can cannellini beans, rinsed and drained in a mesh colander
3 T (45 ml) chopped Italian parsley
1 T (15 ml) extra-virgin olive oil
2 T (30 ml) finely chopped fresh basil, for garnish

Preheat oven to 400 F (200 C) degrees.

Toss the eggplants, bell peppers and onion in a bowl with the garlic, oil, red pepper flakes, salt, and pepper.
Spread on a baking sheet and roast for 30 to 35 minutes (save the bowl to use later). Stir once during roasting.
Meanwhile, lightly brown the nuts in a dry skillet. Do not walk away because they burn easily.

When the eggplant mixture and nuts are cool, transfer them to a food processor fitted with the steel blade. Add the lemon zest, lemon juice, basil, and beans and pulse until the mixture is uniform but still slightly chunky. Spoon into the bowl and stir in the Italian parsley and extra-virgin olive oil.

Transfer to a serving bowl, sprinkle with the chopped basil, and serve with bruschette, crostini, or vegetables.

Bruschette with Tomatoes, Olives & Beans

Bruschette con Pomodori, Olive e Fagioli

This is such an easy antipasto to put together . . . sun-ripened tomatoes, Italian olives, cannellini beans, olive oil, basil, and Italian parsley capture the taste of sunny Italy.

1 French baguette, cut into ½-inch (12-mm) slices
1 (14 oz/398 ml) can cannellini beans, rinsed and drained in a mesh colander
½ cup (125 ml) diced tomatoes
½ cup (125 ml) pitted and chopped Italian black olives
¼ cup (60 ml) extra-virgin olive oil
¼ cup (60 ml) chopped fresh basil
¼ cup (60 ml) chopped Italian parsley
2 cloves garlic, minced
Salt and freshly ground black pepper
6 oz (185 g) soft fresh goat cheese

Bake the bread slices in a 400 F (200 C) degree oven until golden brown; alternatively, grill on top of the stove on a grill pan.

Mix together the beans, tomatoes, olives, olive oil, basil, parsley, and garlic.
Season to taste with salt and pepper.
Spread a layer of goat cheese on each slice of toasted or grilled bread and spoon on the bean mixture.

Bruschette with Mushrooms
Bruschette con Funghi

Here is another bruschetta recipe . . . this time with mushrooms. I like using the combination of cremini mushrooms (baby portobello) and white mushrooms.

1 French baguette, cut into ½-inch (12-mm) slices
3 T (45 ml) extra-light olive oil or grape seed oil
8 oz (250 g) white mushrooms, brushed clean, trimmed and sliced
8 oz (250 g) cremini mushrooms, brushed clean, trimmed and sliced
1 clove garlic, minced
2 t (10 ml) fresh thyme leaves
½ t (2 ml) red pepper flakes
1 large tomato, diced
¼ cup (60 ml) chopped Italian parsley
Salt and freshly ground black pepper

Bake bread slices in a 400 F (200 C) degree oven until golden brown on both sides.
In a large skillet over medium-high heat, heat the oil, add the mushrooms and sauté until golden, about 15 minutes. Add the garlic and cook another minute.
Add the thyme leaves, red pepper flakes, diced tomato, and parsley; season to taste with salt and pepper.
Cook another couple of minutes, then spoon onto the toasted bread slices.

Grilled Polenta with Mushrooms
Polenta Grigliata con Funghi

I find it's so easy and inexpensive to make polenta at home, but you can save some time by purchasing ready-made polenta at your supermarket. It comes rolled into a log and is usually located where gourmet cheeses are sold.

Polenta
4 cups (1 litre) water
2 cups (500 ml) chicken stock
2 t (10 ml) sea salt
1 ¾ cups (435 ml) polenta or coarse-ground yellow cornmeal
3 T (45 ml) unsalted butter
3 T (45 ml) grated Parmigiano-Reggiano cheese
6 oil-packed sun-dried tomatoes, diced (optional)

In a large saucepan, bring the water and chicken stock to a boil, then add the salt.
Slowly add the polenta to the saucepan, whisking as you pour.
Reduce the heat and let the polenta simmer, whisking constantly for about one minute.
Reduce heat to the lowest setting and let simmer for about 15 minutes, stirring often to prevent it from sticking.
Remove from stove, add the butter, grated Parmigiano cheese, and sun-dried tomatoes. Mix well.

Oil a 9-by-13-inch (23-by-33-cm) baking sheet with sides.

Pour the polenta into the prepared baking sheet. Smooth the top evenly with a spatula dipped in cold water. Cover and refrigerate until set, a few hours or up to overnight.

Mushroom Topping
1 lb (500 g) white and cremini mushrooms, brushed clean, trimmed and diced
2 T (30 ml) extra-light olive oil or grape seed oil
1 clove garlic, minced
1 t (5 ml) fresh thyme leaves
1 t (5 ml) chopped fresh oregano
¼ t (1 ml) red pepper flakes
2 Roma tomatoes, diced
Salt and freshly ground black pepper
¼ cup (60 ml) chopped Italian parsley

While the polenta is in the refrigerator, sauté the mushrooms in the oil over medium-high heat, until golden brown. Add the garlic, thyme, oregano, red pepper flakes, and tomatoes; season to taste with salt and pepper.
Cook another minute; remove from heat and stir in most of the parsley (save a little for garnishing).

Remove polenta from refrigerator and turn out onto a cutting board. Cut into about 3-inch (7.5-cm) squares and brush each square with oil. Cook polenta squares on a grill, about 7 to 8 minutes on each side to get dark grill marks. You can also broil them 4-inches (10-cm) from the heat, turning once, until crisp and golden on both sides, about 4 to 5 minutes per side.

Place the polenta slices onto a platter. Spoon mushroom mixture on top.
Sprinkle with the remainder of the parsley and serve warm.

Makes about 12 squares

Cannellini Bean Spread with Rosemary
Crema di Cannellini con Rosmarino

Many of you have had hummus and know it makes a healthy, satisfying snack or lunch. This dip is the Italian version of hummus. Serve with crackers or crostini.

1 (14 oz/398 ml) can cannellini beans, rinsed and drained in a mesh colander
1 small clove garlic, cut in half
1 T (15 ml) extra-virgin olive oil
1 t (5 ml) freshly grated lemon zest
1 T (15 ml) fresh lemon juice
1 T (15 ml) chopped fresh rosemary
¼ t (1 ml) red pepper flakes
Salt and freshly ground black pepper

Place all ingredients in the bowl of a food processor fitted with the steel blade. Process until a smooth paste forms. Taste and adjust the seasoning.
Spoon into a serving bowl and drizzle with a little more extra-virgin olive oil.

Black, Green & Red Olive Tapenade
Tapenade di Olive Nere, Verdi e Rosse

This dish captures the sunny flavors of the Mediterranean. Spread some goat cheese on bruschette or crostini and top with the tapenade. It's also great as a sandwich spread for sliced turkey and dark green lettuce on whole wheat pita pockets.

1 cup (250 ml) pitted black Italian olives, such as Liguria or Gaeta
½ cup (125 ml) pitted red Italian olives, such as Cerignola
½ cup (125 ml) pitted green Italian olives, such as Cerignola
5 to 6 sun-dried tomatoes, in oil
2 T (30 ml) capers, drained and rinsed
2 anchovy fillets, drained, rinsed and patted dry (optional)
2 cloves garlic
2 to 3 large basil leaves
1 t (5 ml) fresh thyme leaves
1 T (15 ml) chopped Italian parsley
1 T (15 ml) fresh oregano leaves
¼ t (1 ml) red pepper flakes
Zest and juice of ½ lemon
1 t (5 ml) red wine vinegar
1 T (15 ml) cognac or other brandy (optional)
¼ cup (60 ml) extra-virgin olive oil

Combine all of the ingredients in the bowl of a food processor fitted with the steel blade. Process to a coarse puree and spoon into a serving bowl.

Salads

"Insalate"

Soups

"Zuppe"

Pasta & Beans
Pasta e Fagioli

This is the classic soup of pasta and beans from Southern Italy, especially popular in Napoli and the Amalfi Coast. Don't be a fool . . . eat pasta fazool! It is truly *amore*.

¼ lb (125 g) pancetta, diced
2 T (30 ml) extra-light olive oil
1 medium onion, diced
2 cloves garlic, minced
½ t (2 ml) red pepper flakes
½ cup (125 ml) dry white wine
2 T (30 ml) tomato paste
2 quarts (2 litres) chicken stock
1 sprig fresh thyme
1 bay leaf
1 (3-inch/7.5-cm) piece Parmigiano-Reggiano cheese rind
2 (14 oz/398 ml) cans cannellini beans with liquid
Salt and freshly ground black pepper
1 cup (250 ml) ditalini or ditali pasta
Extra-virgin olive oil, for drizzling
Freshly grated Parmigiano-Reggiano cheese

In a large pot or Dutch oven, fry the pancetta over medium heat until golden.
Add the oil to the pot and sauté the onion until soft and translucent, about 10 minutes.
Add the garlic and red pepper flakes and sauté another minute.
Add wine and simmer 3 minutes.
Add tomato paste, chicken stock, sprig of thyme, bay leaf, and cheese rind.
Simmer 20 minutes. Add beans and simmer 10 more minutes.
Remove sprig of thyme, bay leaf, and cheese rind; season to taste with salt and pepper.
Add pasta and simmer another 5 to 6 minutes.

Serve with a drizzle of extra-virgin olive oil and some grated Parmigiano cheese.

Serves 4 to 6

Potato, Leek & Gorgonzola Soup
Zuppa di Porri, Patate e Gorgonzola

Autumn and winter are definitely the time for soups and stews. This recipe is a version of potato and leek soup but with an Italian twist . . . gorgonzola cheese! You can leave it out or even try blue cheese. The cooking time is about 30 minutes. Serve with salad and bread or a deli sandwich.

2 T (30 ml) unsalted butter
2 T (30 ml) extra-light olive oil
3 large leeks, cleaned, white part
    diced
1 clove garlic, minced
3 large Yukon Gold or yellow
    potatoes, peeled and cut into
    ½-inch cubes
1 sprig fresh thyme
1 bay leaf
4 cups (1 litre) chicken stock
4 oz (125 g) gorgonzola cheese,
    broken into small pieces
¼ cup (60 ml) dry white wine
1 cup (250 ml) half-and-half
    (half cream) or whole milk
Salt and freshly ground
    black pepper
Italian parsley leaves, for garnish

In a large saucepan, melt the butter and add the olive oil.
Add leeks and sauté for 10 minutes over medium-low heat.
Add garlic and sauté another minute.
Add potatoes, sprig of thyme, bay leaf, chicken stock, and cheese.
Simmer uncovered for 15 minutes.
Stir in wine and simmer another 5 minutes.
Smash some of the potatoes on the sides of the saucepan with a spoon to thicken the soup.
Add the half-and-half or milk and season generously with salt and pepper.

Remove the sprig of thyme and bay leaves. Ladle into soup bowls and garnish with a couple leaves of the parsley.

Note: If you want a smoother soup, after removing the bay leaves and thyme, carefully use an immersion blender to blend the soup to the consistency you like.

Serves 4 to 6

Lentil Soup
Zuppa di Lenticchie

My mother-in-law, Marie, always made lentil soup and served it with pizza. Lentils are a great source of fiber, folate and magnesium. Adding the pasta is optional—the soup tastes just as great without it.

¼ cup (60 ml) extra-light olive oil
1 large onion, diced
2 stalks celery, diced
2 small carrots, peeled and diced
4 cloves garlic, minced
2 cups (500 ml) whole peeled
   Italian tomatoes
3 T (45 ml) tomato paste
4 cups (1 litre) chicken stock
8 cups (2 litres) water
1 bay leaf
1 t (5 ml) freeze-dried or chopped
   fresh basil
1 t (5 ml) freeze-dried or chopped
   fresh oregano
1 cup (250 ml) lentils, rinsed
1 cup (250 ml) ditalini or ditali pasta
Salt and freshly ground black pepper
Freshly grated Parmigiano-Reggiano cheese

In a large pot or Dutch oven, heat the olive oil over medium heat.
Add the onion, celery, and carrots and sauté for 10 minutes. Add garlic and sauté another minute.

Pour the tomatoes into a bowl and hand-crush them, removing the hard center cores.
Alternatively, use an immersion blender to chop the tomatoes.

Add the crushed tomatoes, tomato paste, chicken stock, water, bay leaf, basil, oregano, and lentils to the pot. Bring to a boil, reduce heat, partially cover and simmer for 40 minutes.
Season generously with salt and pepper.

Add the pasta and simmer another 5 to 6 minutes.

Serve with grated Parmigiano cheese and a drizzle of extra-virgin olive oil.

Serves 4 to 6

Quick Tuscan Bean Soup
Zuppa Toscana Veloce con Fagioli (Sciuè Sciuè)

There's nothing like a steaming bowl of hot soup to warm you on a cold autumn or winter evening. This soup is made with canned beans instead of dried beans, making it quick and easy. Any variety of white canned beans will be great with this soup, from the smaller navy bean to the medium great northern bean or the larger cannellini bean.

½ lb (250 g) pancetta, diced
3 T (45 ml) extra-light olive oil
1 large yellow onion, diced
3 cloves garlic, minced
2 sprigs fresh thyme, tied together with
    cotton butcher's twine
2 bay leaves
8 cups (2 litres) chicken stock
3 (14 oz/398 ml) cans great northern or
    any white beans, rinsed and drained
1 (3-inch/7.5-cm) piece Parmigiano-
    Reggiano cheese rind
Salt and freshly ground black pepper
Chopped Italian parsley, for garnish
Freshly grated Parmigiano-Reggiano cheese
Extra-virgin olive oil

In a large pot or Dutch oven, fry the pancetta over medium heat until golden.
Add the oil to the pot and sauté the onion until soft and translucent, about 10 minutes.
Add garlic and sauté another minute.
Add the thyme sprigs, bay leaves, chicken stock, beans, and cheese rind.
Season to taste with salt and pepper and simmer for about 25 minutes.

Remove the thyme sprigs, bay leaves, and cheese rind. Ladle soup into bowls and sprinkle with parsley.
Serve with grated Parmigiano cheese and a drizzle of extra-virgin olive oil.

Serves 4 to 6

Onion Soup with Cheese
Zuppa di Cipolle con Formaggio

Caramelized onions, toasted bread, and melted cheeses are the main components of the classic French onion soup. I decided to make it with Italian cheeses instead. All you need to make this a complete meal is a green salad and, of course, a glass of *vino rosso*. Asiago and fontina cheeses have a nutty flavor and are from the same family as Swiss Emmentaler and Gruyère, making them ideal for this soup.

2 T (30 ml) extra-light olive oil or grape seed oil
4 T (60 ml) unsalted butter
6 large yellow onions, halved and thinly sliced
1 t (5 ml) sugar
4 cloves garlic, minced
¼ cup (60 ml) Marsala wine
4 sprigs fresh thyme, tied together with cotton butcher's twine
2 bay leaves
6 cups (1.5 litre) beef broth
4 cups (1 litre) chicken stock
Salt and freshly ground black pepper
8 oz (250 g) fresh Asiago cheese, sliced
4 oz (125 g) Fontina cheese, sliced
¼ cup (60 ml) freshly grated Parmigiano-Reggiano cheese
1 French baguette or thin loaf Italian bread, cut into ½-inch (12-mm) slices

Heat oil and butter in a large pot or Dutch oven over low heat.
Add onions, cover, and cook for 30 minutes, stirring occasionally.
Remove lid, add sugar and garlic and continue to cook for another 10 minutes, until golden, stirring occasionally.
Add Marsala wine and cook another 5 minutes, to reduce.
Add thyme sprigs, bay leaves, beef broth, and chicken stock; season to taste with salt and pepper.

Bring to a boil, reduce heat, cover, and simmer another 20 minutes.
Remove thyme sprigs and bay leaves.

While soup is simmering, arrange the slices of bread on a baking sheet and bake in a 400 F (200 C) degree oven for about 10 minutes, or until golden brown. Set aside.

Ladle broth and onions into ovenproof soup bowls set on a baking sheet.
Arrange slices of the toasted bread in each bowl so that they cover the soup.
Evenly distribute the cheeses on top.
Heat broiler with rack 6-inches (15-cm) from element. Place baking sheet with bowls of soup under broiler and broil until cheeses are browned and bubbly, about 4 to 5 minutes.
Serve immediately.

Serves 6

Asiago cheese is an Italian cow's milk cheese. Asiago Pressato is fresh and smooth (this is the type used in this recipe). Asiago d'Allevo is crumbly and similar to Parmigiano-Reggiano.

Fontina cheese is made in the Aosta Valley. Italian Fontina can be identified by the stamp of the Matterhorn, and includes the script "FONTINA."

San Francisco Cioppino

Cioppino, pronounced "chuh-Pee-no," is an Italian-American seafood stew made with the catch of the day. San Francisco Italian-Americans invented this recipe in the 1800s, and it must include Dungeness crab. Most countries that border the ocean have their own seafood stew. The French have a Provençal stew called bouillabaisse. In Chile, they have *caldillo de congrio*. In Brazil, it's *moqueca,* and in Positano, Italy, they have *pesce all'aqua pazza* or "fish in crazy water." To save time, you can buy a good quality marinara sauce from your grocery store and cooked Dungeness crabmeat. This recipe serves 2 as a main course and 4 as a first course.

2 cups **Casa Marinara Sauce** (see recipe, page 64) or store-bought marinara sauce

Soffrito "underfried"
2 T (30 ml) extra-light olive oil
1 small leek, cleaned, white part diced
½ carrot, peeled and minced
2 bay leaves
1 clove garlic, minced

In a large pot or Dutch oven, add the olive oil; over low heat, sauté the leek for 5 minutes.
Add the carrot and bay leaves and sauté for another 5 minutes.
Add the garlic and cook another minute. Set aside.

Seafood
1 cooked and cleaned Dungeness crab
12 fresh mussels
12 small fresh clams
½ cup (125 ml) Pinot Grigio or other dry white wine
1 (8 oz/250 ml) bottle clam juice
1 (8 oz/250 g) piece of Pacific cod or other white fish, cut into bite-size pieces
8 large shrimp, peeled and deveined
8 scallops
Salt and freshly ground black pepper
¼ cup (60 ml) chopped Italian parsley
Extra-virgin olive oil, for finishing

Remove the legs from the whole crab, keeping several intact for garnishing the cioppino, if desired. Pick the rest of the crabmeat from the legs and body sections. Set aside (or chill and then bring to room temperature before serving).

If using wild mussels, remove the beards with a pair of "kitchen only" needle-nose pliers.
Scrub the mussels and clams with a brush under cold running water; set aside in a bowl.
Add the wine and clam juice to the pot with the soffrito and heat to a simmer.
Add the mussels and clams and simmer, covered, until they open, about 5 minutes.
Remove the mussels and clams with a slotted spoon and place in a bowl, cover and set aside. Discard any that failed to open.

To the pot, add the Casa Marinara Sauce and simmer for a couple of minutes to heat through.
Add the fish, shrimp, and scallops.
Season to taste with salt and pepper and simmer another 5 minutes.

Remove the bay leaves and divide the cioppino into warmed bowls, leaving some broth in the pan.
Arrange the mussels and clams around the sides of each bowl.
Top with the reserved crabmeat in the center of each bowl and pour the rest of the hot broth over each bowl.

Tuck in the crab legs and sprinkle with parsley and a drizzle of extra-virgin olive oil.
Serve immediately.

Serves 2 to 4

Minestrone

Just about every region of Italy has its own minestrone or "big soup." This was a basic, hearty soup for Italians in the new country. For minestrone alla Genovese, add a dollop of basil pesto sauce on top of the soup. For minestrone alla Milanese, use arborio rice instead of pasta and omit the pesto sauce.

Soffrito "underfried"
¼ lb (125) pancetta, diced
2 T (30 ml) extra-light olive oil
1 medium onion, diced
1 medium leek, cleaned, white part diced
2 stalks celery, diced
3 cloves garlic, minced

In a large pot or Dutch oven, fry the pancetta over medium heat until golden.
Add the oil to the pot and sauté the onion, leek, and celery until soft and translucent, about 10 minutes.
Add garlic and sauté another minute.

Soup

1 (28 oz/796 ml) can whole peeled Italian tomatoes
2 T (30 ml) tomato paste
1 small head savoy cabbage, cored and chopped
1 (3-inch/7.5-cm) piece Parmigiano-Reggiano cheese rind
2 bay leaves
2 sprigs thyme, tied together with cotton butcher's twine
1 t (5 ml) freeze-dried or chopped fresh basil
1 t (5 ml) freeze-dried or chopped fresh oregano
1 T (15 ml) chopped fresh rosemary leaves
12 cups (3 qts/3 litres) chicken stock

3 medium yellow potatoes, peeled and cut into bite-size cubes
3 medium carrots, peeled, cut in half lengthwise and sliced into half moons
2 small zucchini, cut in half lengthwise and sliced into half moons
¼ cup (60 ml) chopped Italian parsley
1 small bunch Swiss chard leaves, trimmed of stems and chopped
1 (14 oz/398 ml) can cannellini beans, rinsed and drained
1 cup (250 ml) ditalini or ditali pasta
Salt and freshly ground black pepper
Freshly grated Parmigiano-Reggiano cheese, for the table

Pour tomatoes into a bowl and hand-crush them, removing the hard center cores.
Alternatively, use an immersion blender to chop the tomatoes.

In the pot with the soffrito, stir in the crushed tomatoes, tomato paste, cabbage, cheese rind,
bay leaves, sprigs of thyme, basil, oregano, rosemary, and chicken stock.
Bring to a boil, lower heat, partially cover and let simmer 30 minutes, stirring a few times.
Add the potatoes and carrots and simmer another 30 minutes.

To the pot, add the zucchini, parsley, Swiss chard, beans, and pasta.
Season to taste with salt and pepper.
Simmer until pasta is al dente, about 5 to 6 minutes.
Remove the cheese rind, bay leaves, and thyme sprigs, before serving.

Sprinkle with a little more parsley and serve with crusty bread and a glass of Pinot Grigio.

Serves 4 to 6

Marie's Beef & Pasta Soup
Zuppa di Pasta con Manzo

This soup served along with pizza was always a favorite dinner at Marie and Ted's house. I remember one time she was in tears when we arrived for dinner. When she strained the soup, she forgot to put another soup pot under the strainer and the broth went down the sink drain. We only had Ted's pizza that night . . . and it was delicious.

Broth
1 T (15 ml) extra-light olive oil or grape seed oil
2 lbs (1 kg) beef shank with marrow bones intact
8 cups (2 litres) boiling water
4 cups (1 litre) beef broth
3 stalks celery with leaves, quartered
4 medium carrots, peeled and quartered
2 medium onions, peeled and quartered
4 garlic cloves, cut in half
2 (28 oz/796 ml) cans whole peeled Italian tomatoes
1 T (15 ml) sugar
1 bunch parsley, rinsed
Freshly grated Parmigiano-Reggiano cheese, for serving

Heat oil in a large soup pot over medium-high heat.
Add the bones with beef shank and brown for 5 minutes on each side.
Add the rest of the above ingredients (except the Parmigiano), cover, and gently simmer for 3 hours.

With a slotted spoon, remove the meat and bones and set them aside to cool.
Strain the broth and vegetables through a sieve into another large soup pot.
Lightly mash the vegetables with a spoon against the sieve to extract the juices and then discard the vegetables or add them to your compost bin.

Remove the lean portions of the meat from the bones. Shred into small pieces and add to the broth in the pot. Discard the bones.

To the broth add:
3 carrots, peeled and cut diagonally into 2-inch (5-cm) chunks
3 sprigs each of thyme and oregano, all tied together with cotton butcher's twine
Salt and freshly ground black pepper
½ lb (250 g) spaghetti, broken into small pieces

Simmer the strained broth for 30 minutes with the carrots and herbs. Season to taste with salt and pepper.
Meanwhile, in a separate pot, cook the pasta until al dente; drain and set aside.
Remove the tied herbs and discard.

Add about ½ cup (125 ml) of the cooked pasta to each soup bowl, then ladle in the soup with some meat and 2 or 3 carrot pieces.

Serve with grated Parmigiano-Reggiano cheese.

Serves 4 to 6

La Bourgogne, July 4th 1898: Sea Disaster

You probably haven't heard about this passenger shipwreck. It happened off of Sable Island, Nova Scotia, on July 4th, 1898, in dense fog at dawn's early light. It occurred 14 years before the infamous *Titanic* disaster. No Hollywood movies were ever made about this disaster—yet 584 souls were drowned. Three were from the Casazza family: Louis (Luigi), his young daughter, Rose, and his brother James (Giacomo). Only one woman survived (Mrs. Adrian LaCasse), and she was saved by her husband.

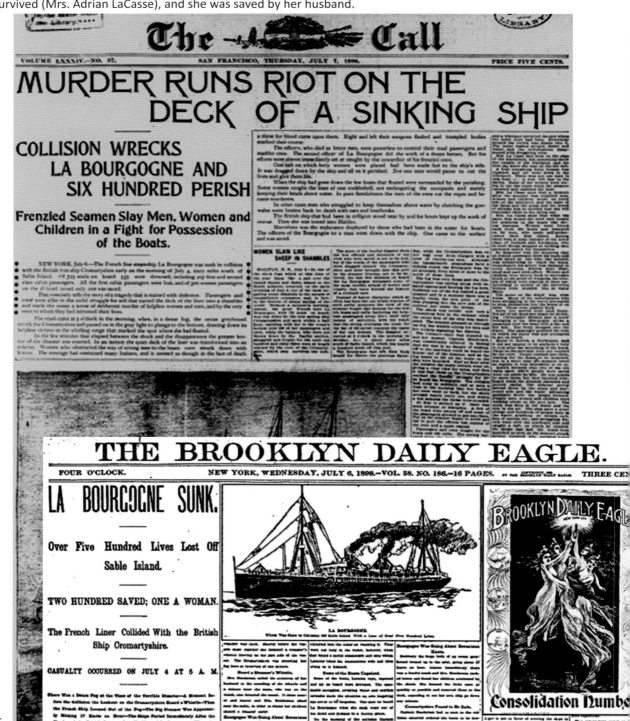

This newspaper article was about Bob's great-grandmother Catherine (Catarina). She was thirty-two years of age at the time of the accident, a wife and mother of five children. When she lost her husband and daughter on that fateful morning, she was left to raise her other children, ranging in age from one to fourteen. It is likely that other Italian-American descendants today may have had ancestors on that doomed ship.

BROOKLYN SPECTATOR, MAY 14, 1965.

At 100 Years, Memories Of an 1898 Sea Tragedy

— Photo by Mr. Photographer

MRS. CATHERINE CASAZZA

By Joseph J. Hasson

In the pre-dawn darkness of July 4, 1898, the French liner La Bourgoyne, with some 700 passengers and crew aboard, was two days out of New York and moving leisurely through the choppy waters off Nova Scotia on her way to Le Havre. The day was to have been one of celebration, at least for the Americans aboard, and the Stars and Stripes would share the spotlight with the Tricolor.

But there was no celebration that day on the Bourgoyne, no flags waving in the sea breeze, no toasts drunk to French and American amity and independence. And to those on land, the day's events brought nothing but sadness.

For, suddenly, out of the murky fog, her outline barely discernible in the haze, came the English trading vessel Cromartyshire, full steam ahead, its course at right angles to the Bourgoyne.

In an instant, there was a sickening, grinding, crushing thud as the Bourgoyne was dealt a death blow amidships by the bow of the Cromartyshire. Five hundred and sixty souls were lost.

THAT WAS 67 years ago. But for a Bay Ridge woman who will celebrate her 100th birthday this Sunday, the tragedy has all the freshness of yesterday.

She is Mrs. Catherine Casazza, who lives at 59 Gelston Ave. with her two daughters, Therese M. and Angela.

Mrs. Casazza lost her husband, Louis, a businessman on his way to a vacation in France, and her brother, James, in that 1898 disaster. She was left a widow with five young children, all of whom she brought up to be happy, healthful, and useful adults. Her reward, and theirs, this Sunday will be the great satisfaction of all of the children being present with their mother on her 100th birthday.

MRS. CASAZZA's three sons are Paul, who lives in Pearl River; Anthony, who lives at 131 74th St. here; and Charles, a retired detective who makes his home in Staten Island. Twelve grandchildren and twenty great-grandchildren round out the family.

Mrs. Casazza was born in New York and has lived almost all of her life in Brooklyn. She was a parishioner in Our Lady of Perpetual Help parish for 55 years before moving to Fort Hamilton ten years ago.

Today, as she approaches the century mark, this remarkable and kindly woman contemplates the future with serenity. In the week ahead she is looking forward to a series of get-togethers with relatives at home. And after that?" "When I'm 106, I think I'll go back to school," she says with a twinkle in her eye.

Pizza & Focaccia

BACK HOME
FOR KEEPS

Casa Pizza Dough

Delicious homemade pizza is easier to make than you think and so much tastier. For best results, make your pizza dough a day before baking the pizza. It slowly rises in your refrigerator, which ensures a golden, crunchy crust with a nice yeasty flavor. This recipe makes one large rectangular pizza or two 12-inch (30-cm) round pizzas. Use a flour with a high gluten content (at least 12% protein).

¾ cup (175ml) lukewarm water
1 t (5 ml) active dry yeast
2 cups (500 ml) unbleached bread flour
1 t (5 ml) fine sea salt
1 t (5 ml) extra-light olive oil

Pour ¼ cup of the lukewarm water into the bowl of an electric mixer fitted with the dough hook. Sprinkle in yeast and let proof for 10 minutes, until the yeast is creamy and foaming.

With the mixer running, slowly add the flour alternating with the rest of the water, salt, and olive oil. Continue to mix until a ball forms, about 10 minutes.

Turn out onto a floured surface and knead for about 10 minutes, until dough is soft and not sticky. Place dough in a large bowl that has been lightly oiled. Spread a little oil on top of the dough, cover with plastic wrap and refrigerate for 24 to 36 hours.

Remove from refrigerator and let bowl with dough come to room temperature before shaping. Divide into 2 balls for round pizzas or leave as one ball for 1 large Sicilian Pizza (see page 54).

Note: When baking pizza at home, I find it easiest to use a two-step process for forming and baking:
Lightly oil two pizza pans and put a ball of dough onto the center of each.
Use your hands to stretch, form, and flatten each ball of dough to a 12-inch round (30-cm). Distribute the toppings on the dough, place one pan on the bottom rack of your preheated oven and bake for about 5 minutes. Then slide the pizza directly onto your preheated pizza stone and bake for another 10 to 12 minutes. Repeat with the second pizza. This parbaking helps avoid sticking—and using a baking stone for the second step does wonders for producing a crisp, golden crust.

(I've never had much success using a baker's peel, but if that works for you, by all means use it!)

Casa Pizza Sauce

This recipe for pizza sauce is so easy to make and can be made a day or two before making the pizza dough. Just cover and refrigerate. The addition of a bunch of fresh basil and a whole onion, cut in half, add flavor but are removed when the sauce is finished—leaving a smooth pizza sauce.

2 (28 oz/796 ml) cans whole peeled Italian tomatoes, preferably D.O.P. San Marzano
¼ cup (60 ml) extra-light olive oil
4 cloves garlic, pushed through a garlic press or minced
½ t (2 ml) red pepper flakes (peperoncino)
2 t (10 ml) freeze-dried or chopped fresh oregano
1 bunch fresh basil, stems included
1 large onion, peeled and cut in half
Salt and freshly ground black pepper

In a large bowl, pour in tomatoes and finely hand-crush them, removing the hard center cores. Alternatively, use an immersion blender to finely chop the tomatoes.

In a large saucepan over medium-low heat, add the oil and garlic and sauté for 1 minute.

Add the crushed tomatoes, red pepper flakes, and oregano to the saucepan and stir to combine.
Tuck in the bunch of basil and onion halves, cut side down.
Season to taste with salt and pepper.
Bring to a simmer and cook, stirring occasionally until thickened, about 30 minutes.

Remove basil and onion halves and discard.

Yields about 4 cups of sauce, enough for 6 to 8 pizzas

Note: This sauce keeps well in the refrigerator for as long as a week and can be frozen for a couple of months.

Rustic Pizza with Roasted Grapes, Prosciutto & Arugula

Pizza con Crudo, Rauco la e Uva Arrosto

Many wood-fired pizza restaurants have a pizza on their menu topped with fresh arugula and Prosciutto di Parma. This rustic, free-form pizza can be served as a main course or cut into small slices for an antipasto. The creaminess of the cheese, the sweetness of the grapes and the saltiness of the prosciutto . . . it's a symphony for your taste buds.

One recipe **Casa Pizza Dough** (see page 50), or use already-prepared pizza dough
30 seedless red grapes
Grape seed oil or extra-light olive oil
Sea salt
8 oz (250 g) French brie cheese or Robiola Piemonte cheese*, cut into small chunks
2 sprigs fresh rosemary, leaves removed and chopped
2 bunches baby arugula, rinsed and dried
¼ lb (125 g) Prosciutto di Parma, thinly sliced
Extra-virgin olive oil, for finishing

Preheat oven to 400 F (200 C) degrees.
Place grapes in a cast-iron skillet or heavy baking pan. Drizzle with a little of the grape seed oil or extra-light olive oil and toss to evenly coat.
Sprinkle with a small amount of sea salt and roast in oven for 15 minutes.
Immediately remove grapes from skillet or baking pan and place in a bowl; set aside.

Raise oven temperature to 425 F (220 C) degrees.

Preheat a pizza stone in middle rack of oven for 15 minutes. Alternatively, you can just bake pizzas on pizza pans or baking sheets.

Lightly oil two pizza pans or baking sheets.

Divide dough into two portions. Use your hands to stretch and form each portion into a rectangular shape. Brush each with some oil.
Divide the cheese chunks evenly between each pizza.
Divide the grapes evenly between each pizza.

Set one pan on the bottom rack of your oven and bake for about 5 minutes.
Slide the crust directly onto the stone and bake for another 10 to 12 minutes, until golden brown; or you can bake on baking sheets or pizza pans for a total of 15 to 17 minutes.

Remove the crust from the oven and add the arugula, prosciutto, and chopped rosemary leaves.
Drizzle with some extra-virgin olive oil and cut the pizza crosswise into strips or serve whole.

Makes 2 pizzas

*Ribiola Piemonte is a fresh cheese from the Piedmont region of Italy that is often used on pizzas and melted into fondues.

Sicilian Pizza

Pizza Siciliana

Sicilian-style pizza, also known as *sfincione* (meaning "thick sponge"), is traditionally baked in a rectanglar pan and cut into square pieces. It is often topped with caramelized onions, bell pepper slices, chopped oives, and sometimes anchovies.

One recipe **Casa Pizza Dough** (see page 50), or use already-prepared pizza dough
One recipe **Casa Pizza Sauce** (see page 51), or use store-bought pizza sauce

Prepare the Casa Pizza Dough one day before you need the pizza. Let the dough come to room temperature before assembling and baking.

The Casa Pizza Sauce can also be made in advance.

1 large sweet onion, cut in half and thinly sliced
2 T (30 ml) extra-light olive oil
2 Italian sausages, casings removed and crumbled
1 bell pepper (any color), seeded and thinly sliced
8 oz (250 g) whole-milk mozzarella cheese, grated
8 oz (250 g) provolone cheese, torn into pieces
½ cup (125 ml) freshly grated Pecorino Romano cheese
1 tin or small jar anchovy fillets, packed in oil (optional)
½ cup (125 ml) pitted and chopped black and green Italian olives
2 T (30 ml) chopped fresh basil

In a skillet over low heat, cook the onion slices in the oil until translucent, about 10 minutes. Spoon into a medium-size bowl and set aside. Add the Italian sausage to the skillet and cook until golden, about 10 minutes. Spoon into the bowl with the onion.
Finally, cook the bell pepper until soft, about 5 minutes. Spoon into the bowl with the onion mixture and toss to combine.

Lightly oil a rimmed 13-by-18-inch (33-by-45-cm) baking pan. Place pizza dough in center of pan. Stretch and flatten to fit, leaving the edges slightly thicker. Set aside and let rise for 30 minutes.

Preheat oven to 425 F (220 C) degrees.

Spread a ladle or two of Casa Pizza Sauce over the dough, leaving a border all around.
Add the onion mixture, then the cheeses, anchovies (if using), and olives.
Bake in center of oven for 25 to 30 minutes.

Sprinkle on the chopped fresh basil and cut into squares.

New York Pizza, Brooklyn Style

My father-in-law, Theodore Robert Casazza, was born and raised in the Bay Ridge section of Brooklyn, New York. His parents were Paul Casazza and Rose Biggio. He loved to make pizzas for the family. Brooklyn-style pizza is well known and loved in New York City; it is unusual because the tomato sauce is not cooked.

One recipe **Casa Pizza Dough** (see page 50), or use already-prepared pizza dough

Uncooked Tomato Sauce
1 (28 oz/796 ml) can whole peeled Italian tomatoes, preferably San Marzano
1 T (15 ml) extra-light olive oil
2 cloves garlic, pushed through a garlic press or minced
1 t (5 ml) sea salt
1 t (5 ml) freeze-dried or chopped fresh oregano
2 t (10 ml) chopped fresh basil
¼ t (1 ml) freshly ground black pepper
½ t (2 ml) red pepper flakes (peperoncino)

Pour tomatoes into a bowl and hand-crush them, removing any hard center cores.
Alternatively, use an immersion blender to finely chop the tomatoes.
Pour into a fine mesh strainer and place over a bowl. Let drain for 30 minutes. Discard the liquid and pour the drained tomatoes back into the bowl.
Add the rest of the ingredients. Stir and let sit on counter, covered, for 1 hour, for flavors to develop.

Toppings
¼ cup (60 ml) freshly grated Parmigiano-Reggiano cheese
8 oz (250 g) whole-milk mozzarella cheese, grated
4 to 5 slices provolone cheese, torn into pieces
2 T (30 ml) chopped fresh basil
Extra-virgin olive oil, for finishing

Preheat oven to 425 F (220 C) degrees.
Lightly oil two pizza pans.

Preheat a pizza stone in middle rack of oven for 15 minutes.

Place a ball of dough onto the center of each pan. Use your hands to stretch, form, and flatten each ball of dough to a 12-inch round (30-cm). See Note on page 50 for details.
Add a ladle of the tomato sauce, sprinkle on a little Parmigiano, some mozzarella and provolone.

Place pizza pan on the bottom rack of oven and bake 5 minutes; then slide the pizza directly onto the heated stone and bake for another 10 to 12 minutes. Repeat with the second pizza.

Garnish with chopped basil, drizzle with a little extra-virgin olive oil, and sprinkle with a little more Parmigiano cheese.

Makes 2 pizzas

Margherita Pizza

Southern Italians know that Napoli is the birthplace of pizza and Sophia Loren . . . in that order, and they are both national treasures. My favorite pizzeria in Napoli is L 'Antica Pizzeria Da Michele, where pizza has been made since 1870. They serve only two kinds: Margherita (named for Queen Margherita), which shows the colors of the Italian flag, and Marinara, which has no cheese but lots of garlic and oregano.

One recipe **Casa Pizza Dough** (see page 50), or use already-prepared pizza dough
One recipe **Casa Pizza Sauce** (see page 51), or use store bought pizza sauce

Parmigiano-Reggiano cheese, grated
8 oz (250 g) fresh mozzarella cheese, sliced
2 t (10 ml) extra-virgin olive oil
Fresh basil leaves, for garnish

Preheat oven to 425 F (220 C) degrees. Lightly oil two pizza pans.
Preheat a pizza stone in middle rack of oven for 15 minutes.

Place a ball of dough onto the center of each pan. Use your hands to stretch, form, and flatten each ball of dough to a 12-inch round (30-cm). See Note on page 50 for details.

Spread a ladle of pizza sauce on the rolled-out pizza dough, leaving a border all around.
Sprinkle with a little Parmigiano cheese and a few slices of the mozzarella cheese.
Place pizza pan on the bottom rack of oven and bake 5 minutes; then slide the pizza directly onto the heated stone and bake another 10 to 12 minutes. Repeat with the second pizza.

Drizzle with olive oil and add a garnish of basil when finished baking.

White Pizza
Pizza Bianca

Most white pizzas are made with ricotta and mozzarella cheeses. This white pizza is made with aged Fontina, provolone, Parmigiano-Reggiano, and Italian black olives.

One recipe **Casa Pizza Dough** (see page 50), or use already-prepared pizza dough
Extra-light olive oil
A few thin slices red onion
8 oz (250 g) Fontina cheese, broken into pieces
8 oz (250 g) provolone cheese, broken up
1 cup (250 ml) pitted and chopped Italian black olives
1 t (5 ml) freeze-dried or chopped fresh oregano
2 cloves garlic, minced
Parmigiano-Reggiano cheese, grated
Fresh rosemary leaves
Extra-virgin olive oil, for finishing

Preheat oven to 425 F (220 C) degrees. Lightly oil two pizza pans.
Preheat a pizza stone in middle rack of oven for 15 minutes.

Place a ball of dough onto the center of each pan. Use your hands to stretch, form, and flatten each ball of dough to a 12-inch round (30-cm). See Note on page 50 for details.
Brush the rolled-out pizza dough with the extra-light olive oil and sprinkle on the red onion slices.
Evenly distribute the cheeses and olives. Sprinkle on the oregano, garlic, and grated cheese.
Place pizza pan on the bottom rack of oven and bake 5 minutes; then slide the pizza directly onto the heated stone and bake another 10 to 12 minutes. Repeat with the second pizza.
Garnish with a few rosemary leaves and a drizzle of extra-virgin olive oil.

Rosemary & Black Olive Focaccia
Focaccia con Olive Nere e Rosmarino

In Ancient Rome, focaccia was a flat bread baked on the health. The basic recipe is thought to have originated with the Etruscans or ancient Greeks. Today it is a flavored flatbread that lends itself to so many options. You can cut it into strips and serve it with soup or cut it into sandwich-size pieces and then cut each in half, lengthwise, for panini (grilled sandwiches).

2 cups (500 ml) lukewarm water
2 ½ t (12 ml) active dry yeast (1 packet)
½ t (2 ml) granulated sugar
½ cup (125 ml) unbleached bread or all-purpose flour

2 T (30 ml) extra-light olive oil
1 t (5 ml) sea salt
4 cups (1 litre) unbleached bread or all-purpose flour
2 T (30 ml) fresh rosemary leaves, chopped and divided

Black Italian olives, pits removed and chopped
Coarse sea salt

Pour the lukewarm water into the bowl of an electric mixer fitted with a dough hook or do this the old fashioned way: in a bowl with a wooden spoon.
Sprinkle in yeast, sugar, and the ½ cup (125 ml) flour.
Mix for a couple of seconds and then set aside to proof; the mixture should be bubbly after 10 minutes.

Add the olive oil and salt, then add the rest of the flour and mix until dough comes to a ball.
This takes about 10 minutes.
Add 1 tablespoon (15 ml) of the rosemary and continue to mix another minute.

Place on a lightly floured surface and knead for about 5 minutes.
Form into a ball and place in a large oiled bowl.
Cover with a pizza pan, kitchen towel, or plastic wrap and let rise in a warm area for 2 hours.

Lightly oil a rectangular 9-by-13-inch (23-by-33-cm) baking pan.
Turn the dough out onto the baking pan, spreading it evenly across the bottom of the pan.
Press the corners of the dough to the sides of the pan to hold.
Cover and set aside in a warm place for 30 to 45 minutes.

Preheat oven to 425 F (220 C) degrees.

With fingertips, gently make dimples in the dough.
Press chopped olives into the dimples and sprinkle with the remaining chopped rosemary and course sea salt; drizzle with a little more extra-light olive oil.

Bake for 20 to 25 minutes, until golden brown.

Brush with a little extra-virgin olive oil, if desired and serve.

Pasta & Gnocchi

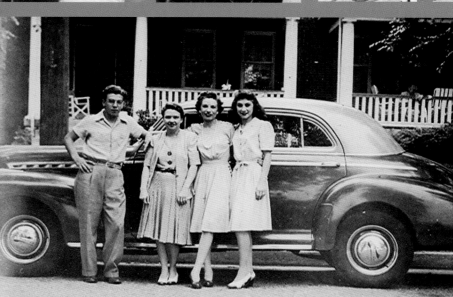

Casa Marinara Sauce

Homemade marinara sauce is very easy and quick to make and tastes much better than even the best supermarket sauce. My marinara sauce is flavored with a small rind of Parmigiano-Reggiano cheese. I love the flavor of basil in the sauce and it is used twice.

¼ cup (60 ml) extra-light olive oil or grape seed oil
1 medium yellow onion, diced
½ t (2 ml) red pepper flakes
6 cloves garlic, thinly sliced
3 (28 oz/796 ml) cans whole peeled Italian tomatoes, preferably D.O.P. San Marzano
1 cup (250 ml) water
2 t (10 ml) freeze-dried or chopped fresh basil
2 t (10 ml) freeze-dried or chopped fresh oregano
½ cup (125 ml) Pinot Grigio or other dry white wine
1 (3-inch/7.5-cm) Parmigiano-Reggiano cheese rind
Salt and freshly ground black pepper
1 T (15 ml) chopped fresh basil

In a large saucepan over medium heat, add the oil and sauté the onion and red pepper flakes for 3 minutes or until translucent. Add the garlic and sauté another minute.

Pour tomatoes into a large bowl and hand-crush them, removing any hard center cores. Alternatively, use an immersion blender to chop the tomatoes.

To the saucepan add the crushed tomatoes, water, basil, oregano, wine, Parmigiano rind, and season to taste with salt and pepper. Simmer, uncovered, for 30 minutes.

Remove the rind with a slotted spoon and discard.
Stir in the tablespoon (15 ml) of chopped fresh basil.

This makes enough sauce for 3 lbs. (1.5 kg) of pasta.

Casa Tomato Sauce

Homemade tomato sauce is easy to make but takes just a little more time than marinara sauce. Traditionally it should include a piece of salt pork or fatback, but I make it with a slice of pancetta. The pancetta is more flavorful than salt pork. You remove it at the end of simmering. I also add a piece of Parmigiano-Reggiano cheese rind to this sauce.

2 oz (60 g) piece of sliced pancetta
2 T (30 ml) extra-light olive oil or grape seed oil
1 medium yellow onion, diced
½ t (2 ml) red pepper flakes
6 cloves garlic, thinly sliced
3 (28 oz/796 ml) cans whole Italian tomatoes, preferably D.O.P. San Marzano
1 cup (250 ml) water
2 t (10 ml) freeze-dried or chopped fresh basil
2 t (10 ml) freeze-dried or chopped fresh oregano
½ cup (125 ml) Pinot Grigio or other dry white wine
1 (3-inch/7.5-cm) piece Parmigiano-Reggiano cheese rind
Salt and freshly ground black pepper
1 T (15 ml) chopped fresh basil

In a large saucepan over medium heat, add the pancetta and sauté for about 5 minutes or until the fat is rendered. Add the oil and sauté the onion and red pepper flakes for 3 minutes or until translucent. Add the garlic and sauté another minute.

Pour tomatoes into a large bowl and hand-crush them, removing any hard center cores. Alternatively, use an immersion blender to chop the tomatoes.

To the saucepan add the crushed tomatoes, water, basil, oregano, wine, Parmigiano rind, and season to taste with salt and pepper. Simmer, uncovered, for 30 minutes.

Remove the pancetta slice and the cheese rind with a slotted spoon and discard.
Stir in the tablespoon (15 ml) of chopped fresh basil.

This makes enough sauce for 3 lbs. (1.5 kg) of pasta.

Spaghetti with Shrimp Fra Diavolo

The word shrimp in Italian is *gamberetto*, but in Italian-American cuisine you will see shrimp *fra diavolo*, "brother devil" or "shrimp from hell." Make it as spicy as you like. The differences between shrimp and prawns are their appearance and the way they reproduce, not necessarily their size. In shrimp (carideans) the sides of the second shell segment overlap the one before and the one after. In prawns (penaeids) the sides of all of the shell segments overlap the segment behind, like roof shingles. Shrimp brood their eggs, while prawns shed their eggs into currents. You will occasionally find female shrimp at the seafood market with eggs intact. A shrimp in the USA is a prawn in Australia, which further confuses us.

I am a firm believer that if you like grated cheese on your pasta with shellfish—do it!

½ cup (125 ml) all-purpose flour
10 to 12 large shrimp, peeled and deveined, tails left on
2 T (30 ml) extra-light olive oil or grape seed oil

2 cups (500 ml) **Casa Marinara Sauce** (see recipe, page 64)
½ to 1 t (2 to 5 ml) red pepper flakes
½ lb (250 g) spaghetti
2 T (30 ml) chopped fresh basil, for garnish
Freshly grated Parmigiano-Reggiano cheese, for serving (optional)

Season flour with salt and pepper and dredge the shrimp in flour. Shake off excess and set aside on a platter.

In a skillet large enough to hold the sauce, shrimp, and pasta, heat 1 tablespoon (15 ml) of the oil over medium heat.
Add half of the shrimp and sauté until they are just beginning to brown, about 2 to 3 minutes.
Remove them with a slotted spoon and set aside on a platter.
Do the same with the other half of shrimp and 1 tablespoon (15 ml) of oil.
Add the Casa Marinara Sauce to the skillet and as much red pepper flakes as desired.
Heat sauce to a simmer.

Meanwhile, boil the spaghetti in salted water for about 7 to 8 minutes, until al dente ("to the tooth"). Before draining, reserve a ladle of pasta water to add to the sauce, if it seems too thick. Pour the spaghetti back into the pot it was boiled in.

After the sauce has been brought to a simmer, add the shrimp and simmer another 2 to 3 minutes to heat the shrimp through.

Pour two ladles of tomato sauce into the pot with the cooked spaghetti and toss to coat with the sauce.

Divide the spaghetti between 2 warm pasta bowls, spoon on some sauce with the shrimp, and garnish with some chopped basil.

Serves 2

Linguine with White Clam Sauce
Linguine alle Vongole Bianche

This recipe has lots of fresh clams and clam juice infused with wine, olive oil, and butter. Serve with crusty bread for sopping up the juices. I like grated Parmigiano cheese on top, but most Italians say that's a "no-no." It's all a matter of preference, and Big Mamma and Mamaw always said "Why not?"

5 to 6 dozen small clams (littleneck or cherrystone)
¼ cup (60 ml) water
1 cup (250 ml) dry white wine, such as Pinot Grigio
1 lb (500 g) linguine
¼ cup (60 ml) extra-light olive oil, divided
1 small yellow onion, diced
4 cloves garlic, thinly sliced
1 t (5 ml) red pepper flakes
1 t (5 ml) freeze-dried or chopped fresh oregano
3 T (45 ml) unsalted butter
Sea salt and freshly ground black pepper
Juice and zest of ½ lemon
½ cup (125 ml) chopped Italian parsley
Extra-virgin olive oil, for finishing
Freshly grated Parmigiano-Reggiano cheese, for serving (optional)

Scrub clams with a brush under cold running water and set aside in a large bowl.

In a large pot that you will boil the pasta in, bring water and wine to a boil.
Add the clams, cover and cook for about 4 to 5 minutes, until clams open.
Discard any that failed to open.

Pour clams and juice from pot into a large mesh strainer set over a large bowl to catch the juices.
Remove about half of the clams from their shells, roughly chop, and place in a smaller bowl.
Leave the rest of the clams in their shells and place in a bowl, covered, to keep warm.
Set the three bowls aside.

Meanwhile, in the same large pot, cook the linguine in boiling, salted water for about 6 to 7 minutes, until al dente. Before draining, reserve two ladles of pasta water: pour one over the clams in their shells to keep them warm, and reserve another ladleful to add to the almost-finished clam sauce.

In a skillet large enough to hold the pasta and sauce, heat the olive oil over medium heat and sauté the onion for about 3 minutes. Add the garlic, red pepper flakes, oregano, and butter and sauté another minute.
Add the chopped clams, clam broth (pour in slowly so that any grit will be left behind), and reserved pasta water. Cook another minute.
Season lightly with salt and pepper and add the lemon zest and juice.
Add the drained pasta to the pan along with the parsley. Heat for just a minute or two while mixing with a spoon, until well combined.

Divide into 4 warm pasta bowls and garnish each bowl with the clams in their shells.
Pour the rest of the hot clam broth from the skillet over each bowl.

Drizzle with a little extra-virgin olive oil and serve with grated Parmigiano cheese, if desired.

Serves 4

Spaghetti, Pirate Style
Spaghetti alla Bucaniera

The Amalfi Coast is a stretch of coastline on the Sorrentine Peninsula in the Province of Salerno in southern Italy. Very ripe little tomatoes called *pendolini* (little hanging ones) are used in making fresh sauces. This pasta dish reminds me of the one I had in the small town of Praiano at the ristorante "Il Pirata," sitting above the emerald water of the Marina di Praia. This is very important: read through the recipe and have everything chopped and set aside, ready to add to the skillet. If you love seafood with pasta, this recipe is for you! You can choose any type of shellfish that you like . . . *frutti di mare del giorno*.

10 fresh mussels
½ lb (250 g) small fresh clams
6 T (90 ml) extra-light olive oil or grape seed oil, divided
½ lb (250 g) medium or large shrimp, peeled and deveined, tails left on
1 large shallot, diced
2 cloves garlic, thinly sliced
1 to 2 t (5 to 10 ml) red pepper flakes
½ cup (125 ml) dry white wine
2 cups (500 ml) cherry tomatoes, cut in half
Sea salt and freshly ground black pepper
½ lb (250 g) spaghetti or linguine
½ lb (250 g) squid, cleaned and cut into ½-inch rings, including tentacles
1 bunch arugula, coarsely chopped
Freshly grated Parmigiano-Reggiano cheese, for serving (optional)

If using wild mussels, remove the beards with a pair of "kitchen only" needle-nose pliers.
Scrub the mussels and clams with a brush under cold running water.

In a large skillet big enough to hold the pasta and sauce, heat half of the oil over medium heat.
Add the shrimp and sauté until the shrimp are pink, about 3 to 4 minutes.
Using a slotted spoon, transfer to a bowl and set aside.

Add the remaining oil to the skillet and sauté the shallot for 3 minutes, or until soft.
Add the garlic and red pepper flakes and cook for another minute.
Add the white wine and tomatoes and simmer for 3 more minutes.
Season to taste with salt and pepper. Turn off heat and set aside.

In a medium saucepan fitted with a lid, add 1-inch (2.5-cm) of water and bring to a boil.
Add the mussels and clams, cover and cook over medium heat for 4 to 5 minutes, or until they open. Scoop the mussels and clams out of the pot with a large slotted spoon into a bowl (save the liquid), discarding any that failed to open. Cover with a plate to keep warm.

In the meantime, boil the pasta in salted water for about 7 to 8 minutes, until al dente.
Drain and set aside, saving about ½ cup (125 ml) of the pasta water to add to the sauce, if needed.

Add about ¼ cup (60 ml) of the shellfish water to the sauce in the skillet and cook another minute.
Add the squid and cook another 2 minutes and then add the arugula.
Add the drained pasta to the sauce and mix, adding the pasta water.
Divide between 2 warm pasta bowls, leaving a little sauce and juice in the skillet.
Arrange the shrimp, mussels, and clams around each plate and pour the sauce and juice on top.
Drizzle with a little extra-virgin olive oil and sprinkle with grated cheese, if desired.

Serves 2

Linguine with Shrimp Scampi & Herbs
Linguine con Gamberi Scampi ed Erbe Aromatiche

I ordered linguine with scampi in a wonderful little restaurant on the Amalfi Coast in an area called Marina di Praia. I thought I was getting regular shrimp with garlic, butter and herbs in a wine sauce. I was surprised because they were little lobsters in their shells and I had to pick through them, but the weather was beautiful and after all . . . we were in Italy! I found out later that they were Norway lobsters or in Italy, *gli scampi*. This recipe is made with wild shrimp and the dish comes together quickly, just chop your shallots, garlic, parsley, and arugula, then zest the lemon and juice it. Set everything aside in individual bowls so it's ready to throw into the skillet. This recipe serves two, but you can easily double the recipe.

½ lb (250 g) linguine
2 T (30 ml) unsalted butter
3 T (45 ml) extra-light olive oil or grape seed oil
1 shallot, cut in half and thinly sliced
2 cloves garlic, thinly sliced
½ t (2 ml) red pepper flakes
1 lb (500 g) large shrimp, peeled and deveined, tails left on
Sea salt and freshly ground black pepper
1 small bunch Italian parsley, stems removed and chopped
1 small bunch arugula, roughly chopped
½ cup (125 ml) dry vermouth or dry white wine
Zest and juice of ½ lemon
Freshly grated Pamigiano-Reggiano cheese (optional)

Cook the pasta in boiling, salted water for about 6 to7 minutes, until al dente. Drain, saving about ½ cup (125 ml) of the water.
In a large skillet, melt the butter with the oil over medium-high heat.
Sauté the shallot, garlic, pepper flakes, and shrimp until the shrimp have just turned pink, about 3 to 4 minutes. Season to taste with salt and pepper, then add the parsley, arugula, wine, lemon zest, and lemon juice. Heat through quickly, stirring to combine.
Add the pasta and pasta water. Toss to combine and add the grated cheese at the table, if desired.

Serves 2

Summer Pasta Salad

Estate Insalata di Pasta

On a warm summer afternoon or evening, nothing could be easier than putting this pasta salad together. Add any vegetable or herb that you like. You can substitute walnuts for the pine nuts (pignoli).

1 lb (500 g) fusilli pasta
2 cups (500 ml) cherry tomatoes, cut in half
1 cup (250 ml) frozen peas, thawed
4 scallions, chopped
2 cloves garlic, pushed through a garlic press or minced
1 cup (250 ml) pitted and chopped Italian black olives
½ cup (125 ml) chopped Italian parsley
1 bunch basil leaves, chopped
1 bunch fresh spinach leaves, chopped
Extra-virgin olive oil, to taste
¼ cup (60 ml) freshly grated Parmigiano-Reggiano cheese
Salt and freshly ground black pepper
½ cup (125 ml) pine nuts, toasted in a dry skillet

Boil fusilli in salted water for about 10 to 11 minutes, until al dente. Drain and place in a bowl to cool. Add all the ingredients except for the pine nuts and toss to combine.
Add the pine nuts at the last minute and toss again.

Serves 4 to 6

Spinach Ravioli with Vodka Cream Sauce

Ravioli di Spinaci con Salsa di Crema di Vodka

You probably wonder why anyone would add an almost tasteless vodka to a sauce. In this recipe the vodka enhances the flavor of the tomatoes. Most supermarkets sell fresh-made ravioli and if you're lucky enough to live near an Italian market, you will be able to find ravioli with different fillings. You can make this recipe with either one of my tomato sauces or use a good-quality store-bought sauce.

One recipe **Casa Marinara Sauce** (see page 64) or **Casa Tomato Sauce** (see page 65)
1 lb (500 g) ravioli

Vodka Cream Sauce
2 cups (500 ml) Casa Marinara Sauce or Casa Tomato Sauce
¼ cup (60 ml) vodka
1 T (15 ml) unsalted butter
½ cup (125 ml) cream or half-and-half (half cream)
Grated Parmigiano-Reggiano cheese
Fresh basil leaves, for garnish

In a skillet large enough to hold the ravioli and sauce, add the 2 cups Casa Marinara Sauce or Casa Tomato Sauce and vodka. Simmer 10 minutes.
Remove from heat and add the butter and cream or half-and-half and stir in.

While the vodka sauce is simmering, boil the ravioli in salted water just until they rise to the top of the water. Lift ravioli out with a large slotted spoon and add directly to the skillet with the vodka cream sauce.

Serve with the grated Parmigiano cheese and garnish with fresh basil leaves.

Serves 2 to 4

Spaghetti al Pesto Genovese

Pesto is a sauce originating in Genoa, in the Liguria region of northern Italy. Pesto Amalfitana is made with Italian parsley in place of basil, and walnuts in place of pine nuts (pignoli). If you want a creamier pesto, add one small peeled and boiled potato along with the rest of the ingredients in the blender.

4 cups fresh basil leaves, packed
¼ cup (60 ml) pine nuts or walnuts, toasted in a dry skillet until lightly golden
4 cloves garlic, peeled
2 T (30 ml) fresh lemon juice
1 (2-inch/5-cm) chunk Parmigiano-Reggiano cheese, cut up
1 (1-inch/2.5-cm) chunk Pecorino Romano cheese, cut up
1 cup (250 ml) extra-virgin olive oil
1 lb (500 g) spaghetti or other pasta
Salt and freshly ground black pepper
Fresh basil leaves, for garnish

In a food processor fitted with the steel blade, add the basil, nuts, garlic, lemon juice, and cheeses; process until smooth. While machine is running, add the olive oil in a slow, steady stream and process to make a smooth paste.
Cook pasta in boiling salted water for 7 to 8 minutes, until al dente.
Save about ½ cup (125 ml) of the pasta water before draining.
Pour pasta back into pan, add some of the pesto, and season to taste with salt and pepper.
Add a little of the pasta water to slightly thin the sauce, if needed.
The pesto can be frozen in small plastic baggies or kept in the refrigerator for up to 5 days.

Serves 4

Gnocchi alla Sorrentina

In Italian, gnocchi means "lump" or "knot." The first time I had Gnocchi alla Sorrentina was at Ristorante Il Pino in Praiano, on the Amalfi Coast of Italy. The people of Positano say, "The best thing about that restaurant is the view . . . OF POSITANO!" There is a bit of a rivalry between the two towns. I have made gnocchi (NYOK-kee) a couple of times, but you can buy it in the fresh pasta section of most grocery stores.

2 cups **Casa Marinara Sauce** (see recipe, page 64) or **Casa Tomato Sauce** (see recipe, page 65)
1 lb (500 g) fresh potato gnocchi
2 T (30 ml) grated Parmigiano-Reggiano cheese
1 (8 oz/250 g) ball fresh mozzarella (or use bocconcini, if available), cut into pieces
Fresh basil leaves, for garnish

In a large skillet, heat the tomato sauce and add the Parmigiano cheese.

Bring a large pot of salted water to a boil.
Drop in all of the gnocchi and boil until they rise to the surface, then boil one minute longer.
Lift out the gnocchi with a large slotted spoon, add to the skillet and gently toss.
Add the mozzarella and gently toss again to combine.

Serves 4

Bucatini with Garlic & Oil
Bucatini con Aglio e Olio

Big Mamma and Papa Greco's first child was Elisabeth (Elisabetta), born in New York City in 1899. This recipe comes from Elisabeth Greco Noviello, known as "Mamaw."

It is important to make your own bread crumbs for this recipe. This dish is well known in Sicily and Abruzzo. You can use bucatini, spaghetti or linguine, whichever you prefer.

It was a favorite of my husband's sister, Joan Elizabeth Casazza Koliopoulos. Rest in peace, Joan.

1 lb (500 g) bucatini, spaghetti or linguine
3 slices Italian or sourdough bread, preferably day-old
1 cup (250 ml) chopped Italian parsley
½ cup (125 ml) extra-light olive oil
3 to 4 anchovy fillets
4 cloves garlic, thinly sliced
1 t (5 ml) red pepper flakes
2 t (10 ml) lemon zest
Salt and freshly ground black pepper
Pecorino Romano cheese, grated
Extra-virgin olive oil, for finishing

Bring a large pot of water to a boil, add some salt, and cook bucatini for about 11 to 12 minutes (spaghetti for 7 to 8 minutes, linguine for 6 to 7 minutes), until al dente.
Drain pasta, reserving 2 cups (500 ml) of the pasta water.

Tear bread into pieces and place in a food processor fitted with the steel blade; process until finely crumbled.

In a skillet large enough to hold all of the pasta, toast the bread crumbs until golden, stirring constantly. Do not walk away, because they will burn.
Set aside in a bowl and stir in the chopped parsley.

In the same skillet, heat the oil over medium heat. Add the anchovies and cook a couple of minutes while breaking them up with a wooden spoon until you can't recognize that they are anchovies any longer.

Add the garlic and red pepper flakes and cook for about 2 minutes. Do not let the garlic brown.
Remove skillet from heat and add the reserved pasta water.
Place back on the heat and simmer for 2 minutes to reduce slightly.
Add lemon zest and season to taste with salt and pepper.
Add the pasta to the pan and mix well.

Twirl with a pasta server or carving fork and place into warmed pasta bowls.
Sprinkle with the bread crumb mixture.
Serve with a little more grated cheese and a drizzle of extra-virgin olive oil.

Serves 4

Casarecce with Pancetta & Tomato Sauce
all'Amatriciana

In Rome this tomato sauce is served with bucatini, which is a hollow version of spaghetti; it's like a straw with a tiny hole. It comes from the Italian word *buco,* meaning hole. In the small town of Amatrice, which is about 80 miles (129 km) northeast of Rome, they prefer spaghetti. This time I made it with *casarecce* (cah-sah-reck-ee) pasta, which translates to "homemade." You can use any pasta that you like. This sauce is so flavorful because of the pancetta. If you can't find pancetta, unsmoked bacon makes a good substitute. Either way you will enjoy having extra sauce for another meal.

8 oz (250 g) pancetta, diced
2 T (30 ml) extra-light olive oil or grape seed oil
1 medium yellow onion, diced
½ t (2 ml) red pepper flakes
4 cloves garlic, pushed through a garlic press or minced
3 (28 oz/796 ml) cans whole peeled Italian tomatoes
1 cup (250 ml) water
1 T (15 ml) freeze-dried or chopped fresh basil
2 t (10 ml) freeze-dried or chopped fresh oregano
½ cup (125 ml) Pinot Grigio or other dry white wine
Salt and freshly ground black pepper
1 lb (500 g) casarecce or pasta of your choice
¼ cup (60 ml) freshly grated Parmigiano-Reggiano cheese

Fresh basil leaves, for garnish
Freshly grated Parmigianno-Reggiano cheese

In a large saucepan over medium heat, add the pancetta and sauté for about 5 minutes or until the fat is rendered. Add the oil and sauté the onion and red pepper flakes for 3 minutes or until translucent. Add the garlic and sauté another minute.

Pour tomatoes into a large bowl and hand-crush them, removing any hard center cores. Alternatively, use an immersion blender to chop the tomatoes.

To the saucepan add the crushed tomatoes, water, basil, oregano, wine, and season to taste with salt and pepper. Simmer, uncovered, for 30 to 40 minutes.

Meanwhile, boil the pasta in salted water until al dente, being sure to save a little of the pasta water to add to the sauce, if it seems too thick.

When sauce has finished simmering, stir in the grated Parmigiano cheese.

Pour drained pasta back into the pot and add some of the tomato sauce, as needed.
Spoon pasta into warm pasta bowls, sprinkle on a little more cheese and garnish with basil.

This makes enough sauce for 3 lbs. (1.5 kg) of pasta.

Serves 4

Penne alla Norcina

Norcia, in the mountains of southeastern Umbria, is known for its black truffles and pork. In fact, Norcia is the pork capital of Italy. The shop of a pork butcher anywhere in Italy is called a *norcineria*. Since black truffles are hard to find and very expensive, you can look for black truffle oil in the gourmet section of your supermarket. A little bottle will last a long time and is so worth it. Use fresh thyme—if you don't have it, leave it out. Get the best quality Italian sausages you can find.

2 T (30 ml) extra-light olive oil or grape seed oil
8 oz (250 g) cremini and/or button mushrooms, cleaned, trimmed, and sliced
1 small onion, cut in half and thinly sliced
2 cloves garlic, thinly sliced
1 lb (500 g) mild or hot Italian sausages (about 5 to 6 links), removed from casings
1 cup (250 ml) dry white wine
1 ½ cups (375 ml) whole milk
2 sprigs of thyme, leaves stripped from stems
Salt and freshly ground black pepper
1 lb (500 g) penne pasta
1 cup (250 ml) frozen peas, thawed
2 T (30 ml) black truffle oil
¼ cup (60 ml) chopped Italian parsley
½ cup (60 ml) freshly grated Parmigiano-Reggiano cheese

In a skillet or pot large enough to hold the sauce and pasta, heat the oil over medium heat and cook the mushrooms until golden brown.
Lower the heat and add the onion and sauté 5 minutes.
Add garlic and sauté another minute.

Transfer the mushroom mixture to a bowl and set aside.
Raise the heat back to medium and add the sausages. Break them into small pieces with a wooden spoon while they cook.
Once the sausage has browned, add the wine and simmer for a couple of minutes.
Add the milk and thyme; season to taste with salt and pepper.
Continue to cook over very low heat, stirring, until the sauce has thickened slightly, about 5 minutes.

During this time, bring a large pot of salted water to a boil and cook penne for 8 to 9 minutes, until al dente. Drain the penne but save ½ cup (125 ml) of the pasta water.

After sauce has simmered 5 minutes, return the mushroom mixture to the skillet or pot, add the peas and truffle oil, and continue to simmer another minute.
Add the drained pasta, Italian parsley, and Parmigiano cheese.
Add some of the reserved pasta water to slightly thin the sauce, if needed.

Ladle into warm pasta bowls and serve with additional grated Parmigiano cheese.

Serves 4

Spaghetti alla Puttanesca

In the Italian language a *puttana* is a "lady of the night." This pasta dish is quick and easy to make, and perhaps that's how it got its name—because the ladies of the night could make it quickly between customers. I mash the anchovies along with garlic in a mortar and pestle, and it gives that wonderful flavor without being overpowering. If you want a stronger anchovy flavor, use one or two more. You can find the Italian olives in most supermarkets and, of course, at any Italian market.

¼ cup (60 ml) extra-light olive oil or grape seed oil
1 medium onion, diced
1 ½ cups (375 ml) pitted and chopped Italian green olives, preferably cerignola or castelvetrano
1 cup (250 ml) pitted and chopped Italian black olives, preferably gaeta or lugano
¼ cup (60 ml) capers, drained
3 to 4 anchovies, mashed in a mortar and pestle or use about 1 T (15 ml) anchovy paste
4 cloves garlic, mashed in a mortar and pestle or minced
½ cup (125 ml) Italian white wine (Frescati, Orvieto, or Pinot Grigio)
2 (28 oz/796 ml)) cans whole peeled Italian tomatoes
1 ½ lbs (750 g) spaghetti
½ t (2 ml) red pepper flakes
Salt and freshly ground black pepper
¼ cup (60 ml) chopped Italian parsley
1 T (15 ml) chopped fresh basil
Fresh basil leaves, for garnish
Freshly grated Parmigianno-Reggiano cheese

In a large pot, sauté the onions in the oil over medium-low heat for 5 minutes until translucent.
Add olives, capers, mashed anchovies, and garlic and sauté another minute.
Add the wine and simmer for a couple of minutes.

Pour tomatoes into a large bowl and hand-crush them, removing the hard center cores.
Alternatively, use an immersion blender to chop the tomatoes.

Add the crushed tomatoes to the pot and simmer for about 25 minutes.

Meanwhile, bring a large pot of salted water to a boil, add the spaghetti and cook 7 to 8 minutes, until al dente. Drain the spaghetti, but save ½ cup (125 ml) of the pasta water.

Add some of the reserved pasta water to slightly thin the sauce, if needed.

Season to taste with red pepper flakes, salt, and pepper.
Add the chopped parsley, basil, and drained pasta; toss to coat.

Garnish with basil and serve with grated Parmigiano cheese.

Serves 6

Spaghetti alla Carbonara

I prefer spaghetti carbonara made with unsmoked bacon instead of pancetta. If you are a purist, make it with *guanciale* "gwan-CHAL-lay" (pork cheeks) or pancetta. Authentic spaghetti alla carbonara does not contain cream. The creaminess comes from the eggs and cheese. Grate the cheeses, slice the shallots and garlic first, and set them aside on a cutting board. This is my son Brandon's favorite. We lived near an Italian restaurant in Washington, D.C., and he always ordered this when we ate there. But why go to a restaurant for this when you can make it to perfection at home?

8 oz (250 g) unsmoked bacon (or use guanciale or pancetta), diced
2 T (30 ml) extra-light olive oil
2 T (30 ml) unsalted butter
2 medium shallots, cut in half and thinly sliced
2 cloves garlic, thinly sliced
½ cup (125 ml) dry white wine

1 lb (500 g) spaghetti
3 whole eggs and 2 egg yolks
½ cup (125 ml) freshly grated Parmigiano-Reggiano cheese
½ cup (125 ml) freshly grated Pecorino Romano cheese
Freshly ground black pepper
1 t (5 ml) red pepper flakes
1 T (15 ml) chopped Italian parsley
Thinly shaved Parmigiano or Pecorino cheese, for garnish

In a large skillet that is big enough to hold the cooked pasta, cook the bacon until crisp.
Pour out most of the fat and add the olive oil and butter; sauté the shallots for about 2 minutes.
Add the garlic and sauté another minute.
Add the wine and stir with a wooden spoon, scraping up the flavorful brown particles from the bacon. Turn off the heat and set aside.

Bring a large pot of salted water to a boil, add the spaghetti and cook 7 to 8 minutes, until al dente. Drain the spaghetti, but save 1 cup (250 ml) of the pasta water.

While the pasta is cooking, put the eggs and yolks into a mixing bowl. Add half of the grated cheeses and season to taste with black pepper and red pepper flakes. Whisk until well combined. Return the skillet with bacon mixture to low heat. Add the hot drained spaghetti to the pan and toss for a couple of minutes to incorporate.

Remove the skillet from the burner and pour the egg-cheese mixture onto the pasta, tossing quickly and thoroughly, which will gently cook the eggs using the heat of the pasta.

Return the skillet to low heat and toss another minute.
Add some of the reserved pasta water to slightly thin the sauce.
Add the chopped parsley, garnish with some shaved cheese and serve.

Serves 4

Gnocchi alla Sardinia

Sardinia, the second largest island in the Mediterranean, is known for its excellent pork. Sardinia is one of the rare places in the world known as a "Blue Zone," where people often live past 100. Buy a package of gnocchi in your grocery store and make this sauce. It is the same sauce I use for Pappardelle with Italian Sausage Sauce (see page 96). The recipe for the sausage sauce makes enough for eight servings, and it freezes well.

Italian Sausage Sauce
1 lb (500 g) mild or hot Italian sausages (about 5 to 6 links)
1 cup (250 ml) good dry Italian wine, such as Frascati, Orvieto, or Pinot Grigio
¼ cup (60 ml) extra-light olive oil or grape seed oil
1 medium onion, diced
3 cloves garlic, pushed through a garlic press or minced

2 (28 oz/796 ml) cans whole peeled Italian tomatoes
1 t (5 ml) freeze-dried or chopped fresh oregano
1 t (5 ml) chopped fresh basil
Salt and freshly ground black pepper
1 lb (500 g) potato gnocchi
Fresh basil leaves, for garnish
Freshly grated Parmigiano-Reggiano cheese

Remove sausage from casings and place in a large bowl.
Pour in ¼ cup (60 ml) of the wine and crush with hands until the sausage is in small pieces.
The wine makes it easier to break up the sausage.

Heat oil in a large pot or Dutch oven. Add onion and sauté for 5 minutes.
Add garlic and sauté another minute.

Add the sausages and cook for about 5 minutes, breaking up pieces with a wooden spoon.
Add the rest of the wine and cook until the wine has mostly evaporated.

In the same large bowl, pour in the tomatoes and hand-crush them, removing the hard center cores. Alternatively, use an immersion blender to chop the tomatoes.

Add the crushed tomatoes to the pot along with the oregano and basil.
Season to taste with salt and pepper and simmer 30 minutes.

Bring a large pot of salted water to a boil. Cook the gnocchi, stirring gently, until tender (about one more minute after they rise to the surface).
Drain the gnocchi, but save ½ cup (125 ml) of the pasta water for thinning the sauce, if needed.
Pour gnocchi back into the empty pot.
Mix in some of the sauce and serve with a little more sauce on top.
Garnish with some basil leaves and grated Parmigiano cheese.

Serves 4

Frascati wine comes from the Lazio city of the same name. Known as the "City of Wine," Frascati is not far from Rome. The Romans called this wine the "Gold Wine" not only for its golden color but in reference to the money it brought to the local economies.

Orvieto wine comes from the Umbrian city of the same name. The Etruscans knew that this area was perfect for grape growing. Orvieto was called "Liquid Gold" and was the wine of choice for popes and kings.

Pinot Grigio wine comes from the northeast regions of Veneto and Friuli and is light and crisp. Pinot translates to "pine cone" and is named that because of the characteristic pine cone shape of the bunch of grapes. Grigio translates to "gray." It is Italy's most popular white wine.

Casazza Easy Spaghetti & Meatballs

It's sometimes difficult to find a good bowl of spaghetti and meatballs in Italian-American restaurants. Usually the sauce (gravy) is too acidic and the meatballs are gray in color. I make Big Mamma's Sunday Gravy once or twice a year with Italian sausages, meatballs, and ribs. It simmers on the stove for 5 hours, but this recipe is much faster and lighter. If I had a restaurant, this would definitely be on the menu. As an option, you can substitute ½ pound (250 grams) of ground veal for ½ pound (250 grams) of the ground beef.

Meatballs
3 slices Italian bread, preferably day-old
3 T (45 ml) milk
1 ½ lbs (750 g) lean ground beef
½ lb (250 g) ground pork
2 large egg yolks
¼ cup (60 ml) minced Italian parsley
1 t (5 ml) garlic powder
½ t (2 ml) onion powder
1 cup (250 ml) freshly grated Parmigiano-Reggiano cheese
Salt and freshly ground black pepper

Tear up the bread and process in a food processor until finely crumbled.
In a large bowl, combine the bread crumbs with the milk and stir to combine.
Set the mixture aside until the crumbs have absorbed the milk.
Add the remaining ingredients, and with dampened hands, shape into 1 ½-inch (3.80-cm) balls.

In a large heavy pot or Dutch oven, heat a little extra-light olive oil until hot, but not smoking.
Adjust heat to medium-low and slowly fry meatballs in batches until brown on all sides.
Do not attempt to turn meatballs until they are thoroughly brown on one side and easily release from the bottom of the pan. Be patient with this step or you will have odd-shaped meatballs.
Using a slotted spoon, transfer to a large bowl and set aside while frying the rest.

"Quick Sunday Gravy"

3 (28 oz/796 ml) cans whole peeled Italian tomatoes
1 large onion, diced
4 cloves garlic, pushed through a garlic press or minced
½ cup (125 ml) dry red wine
1 (24 oz/750 ml) can tomato sauce
½ t (2 ml) red pepper flakes
1 T (15 ml) granulated sugar (optional)
1 t (5 ml) freeze-dried or chopped fresh oregano
2 t (10 ml) freeze-dried or chopped fresh basil
Salt and freshly ground black pepper
1 lb (500 g) spaghetti
Chopped fresh basil, for garnish
Freshly grated Parmigiano-Reggiano cheese

Pour tomatoes into a large bowl and hand-crush them, removing the hard center cores.
Alternatively, use an immersion blender to chop the tomatoes.

In the same large heavy pot or Dutch oven, pour out some of the excess fat (but not the brown particles) and add a little more extra-light olive oil.
Over medium-low heat, sauté the onion for 10 minutes.
Add the garlic and continue to sauté another minute. Add the wine and simmer a few seconds.
Pour the crushed tomatoes into the pot and scrape up any browned particles from the bottom of the pot. Pour in the tomato sauce, red pepper flakes, sugar, oregano, and basil.
Season to taste with salt and pepper. Partially cover and simmer 1 hour.

Add the meatballs and simmer, partially covered, another 45 minutes, gently stirring occasionally.

Boil the spaghetti in salted water for 7 to 8 minutes, until al dente.
Drain well, then add the spaghetti back into the pot.
Mix in some of the sauce to color the spaghetti and serve with a little more sauce, some meatballs, chopped basil, and grated cheese.

Serves 4

* You should have 28 to 32 meatballs with extra sauce for another meal.

Sunday Rigatoni with Beef Shank Gravy

Here is a hearty Sunday Italian-American dinner from Mamaw. The beef is so tender and the marrow bones give the gravy so much flavor. *Buona domenica a tutti!*

2 (28 oz/796 ml) cans whole peeled Italian tomatoes
2 lbs (1 kg) beef shank with marrow bones intact
2 T (30 ml) extra-light olive oil or grape seed oil, divided
1 medium onion, diced
4 oz (125 g) pancetta or unsmoked bacon, diced
4 cloves garlic, thinly sliced
2 T (30 ml) tomato paste
½ cup (125 ml) dry red wine or water
½ t (2 ml) red pepper flakes
Salt and freshly ground black pepper
2 T (30 ml) chopped fresh basil
1 lb (500 g) rigatoni
Chopped fresh basil, for garnish
Freshly grated Grana Padano* or Parmigiano-Reggiano cheese

Pour tomatoes into a large bowl and hand-crush them, removing the hard center cores.
Alternatively, use an immersion blender to chop the tomatoes.

In a large heavy pot or Dutch oven, brown the beef shanks in a tablespoon of oil for about 6 to 7 minutes on each side. Do not turn the shanks until they are deeply browned. This will add flavor and allow the meat to release from the pan. Remove the meat from the pot and set aside.

Pour off any excess grease and add the rest of the oil.
Sauté the onion and pancetta for about 10 minutes over low heat.
Add the garlic and sauté another minute.

Add the crushed tomatoes, tomato paste, wine or water, red pepper flakes, and season to taste with salt and pepper.
Simmer for 10 minutes, then return the beef shanks to the pan and nestle them into the sauce.
Cover with a tight-fitting lid and place in a 325 F (170 C) degree oven for 2 to 2 ½ hours.
Using tongs, transfer the beef shanks to a cutting board.
When cool enough to handle, shred the meat and place back into the pot.
Discard the marrow bones. Reheat gravy and stir in chopped basil.

Boil the rigatoni in salted water for about 9 to 10 minutes, until al dente.
Drain rigatoni and pour back into the pot.
Add a couple of ladles of the gravy (with some shredded meat) to the pasta and toss.
Spoon into warm pasta bowls, add a little more of the gravy and meat to the top of the pasta.
Sprinkle with some chopped basil and serve with grated cheese.

Serves 4

* Grana Padano cheese is one of the world's first hard cheeses; it was made by monks near Milan, Italy, in the 12th century. *Grana* means "grain" in Italian, referring to the texture of the cheese.

Florentine Meatballs
Polpette alla Fiorentina

Back in the early 1970s, we had a group of friends who also loved to cook. We would have amazing dinner parties that lasted until the wee hours of the morning. We were the only couple who had a baby at that time. We would bring him and place him on the hosts' bed with pillows all around him. At one of our gatherings, a friend who had lived in Florence for a while with an Italian family made this delicious Florentine meatball recipe.

As an option, you can substitute ½ pound (250 grams) of ground veal for ½ pound (250 grams) of the ground beef.

1 medium onion, peeled and cut into chunks
1 stalk celery, cut into chunks
1 medium carrot, peeled and cut into chunks
1 clove garlic
1 lb (500 g) lean ground beef
½ lb (250 g) ground pork
1 large egg yolk
½ cup (125 ml) freshly grated Parmigiano-Reggiano cheese
¼ cup (60) bread crumbs, preferably homemade
2 T (30 ml) minced Italian parsley
1 t (5 ml) fresh thyme leaves
½ t (2 ml) ground nutmeg
Salt and freshly ground black pepper

1 cup (250 ml) flour
¼ cup (60 ml) extra-light olive oil or grape seed oil
1 cup (250 ml) dry red wine
3 cups (750 ml) beef broth

1 lb (500 g) pappardelle, tagliatelle, or fettucine
Lemon wedges
Chopped Italian parsley, for garnish
Grated Parmigiano-Reggiano cheese

Place onion, celery, carrot and garlic in the bowl of a food processor.
Process until finely diced; alternatively, you can mince with a knife.
In a large bowl, mix the vegetables with the ground beef, ground pork, egg yolk, grated cheese,
bread crumbs, parsley, thyme, and nutmeg. Season to taste with salt and pepper.
Form into medium-size meatballs.

Gently roll the meatballs in flour and set aside on a platter or baking sheet.
In a large heavy pot or Dutch oven, heat half of the oil over medium heat and brown meatballs in
two batches. Let the meatballs brown on one side for about 5 to 6 minutes before turning.
This way the meatballs will not break apart. They will let go of the bottom of the pan when brown.
Using a slotted spoon, transfer the meatballs to a large bowl.

Add the wine and beef broth to the pan and scrape up any browned particles from the bottom of
the pot. Return the browned meatballs to the pot and bring to a simmer. Cover, turn heat to the
lowest setting, and slowly simmer for 1 ½ hours, stirring once halfway through the cooking time.
Boil the pasta in salted water, until al dente. Drain pasta and divide into warm pasta bowls.
Spoon 5 to 6 meatballs on top of each bowl of pasta and ladle on some of the reduced beef broth.
Serve with lemon wedges, chopped parsley, and grated cheese.

Serves 4

Pappardelle with Italian Sausage Sauce
Pappardelle al Ragú di Salsiccia

I have made pappardelle pasta several times by hand and have found that you don't need a pasta machine. The recipe for the sausage sauce makes enough for eight servings, and it freezes well. Serve this with either pappardelle, tagliatelle, or potato gnocchi. This is the same recipe I use for Gnocchi alla Sardinia (see page 88).

One recipe for **Italian Sausage Sauce** (see page 88)
1 lb (500 g) dried pappardelle, or make the Hand-Made Pasta Dough (recipe follows)
3 T (45 ml) chopped fresh basil, for garnish
Freshly grated Parmigiano-Reggiano cheese

Hand-Made Pasta Dough (no pasta machine, processor or mixer required)
2 cups (500 ml) all-purpose flour, plus more for dusting
¾ cup (175 ml) semolina flour
4 large eggs
2 t (10 ml) kosher or sea salt
1 T (15 ml) extra-virgin olive oil
Semolina flour, for final dusting

On a large clean work surface, sift the two flours together into a pile and make a well in the center.

Crack eggs into the well and add the salt and olive oil.
Using a fork, gently whisk together the eggs and then gradually pull in the flour from all sides
with the fork until it all comes together to form a dough.

Knead by hand for 5 minutes.
Place a bowl over the dough and let rest on the counter for 15 minutes.
Wrap the dough in plastic wrap, flatten slightly, and refrigerate for at least 1 hour.

Place the dough back on a lightly floured surface and dust with flour.
Starting in the center of the dough, using a rolling pin, roll away from you while turning the dough
occasionally. Try to roll it into a rectangle so thin that you can almost see through the dough.
Let dry for 10 minutes, then lightly dust top of dough with flour and loosely roll up into a cylinder.

With a sharp knife, cut into about ¾-inch (18-mm) slices for pappardelle and a little narrower slices
for tagliatelle.
Unroll the strips and toss with semolina flour to separate.
Loosely place each strip on a sheet pan in a clump and cover with a clean, damp, tea towel until
ready to cook.

Bring a large pot of salted water to a boil, add the pasta and cook 3 to 4 minutes, until al dente.
Drain and pour the pasta back into the pot and mix with some of the sauce.
Serve with a little more sauce on top, some chopped basil leaves, and grated cheese.

Serves 4

Pappardelle translates to "gobble up"
Tagliatelle translates to "to cut"
Fettuccine translates to "little ribbons"

Big Mamma's Orecchiette alla Picerno

Teresa Lapetina, "Big Mamma," was from the village of Picerno (Pee-chair-no). It is located in the province of Potenza in the southern region of Basilicata. This village is known for its *salumi* (cold meats) and Pecorino Romano cheese, which is a hard, salty cheese. *Pecora* means "sheep" in Italian and *orecchiette* translates to "little ears." The meatballs are very small—they're just a little larger than the size of the cooked pasta. As an option, you can use ½ pound (250 grams) each of ground beef, pork, and veal. *Tutti a tavola a mangiare!*

Meatballs
3 slices Italian bread, preferably day-old
2 T (30 ml) milk
¾ lb (375 g) lean ground beef
¾ lb (375 g) ground pork
½ t (2 ml) garlic powder
1 large egg yolk
2 T (30 ml) minced Italian parsley
Salt and freshly ground black pepper
¼ cup (22 g) freshly grated Pecorino Romano cheese

2 T (30 ml) extra-light olive oil or grape seed oil, for frying

3 cups **Casa Marinara Sauce** (see recipe, page 64) or **Casa Tomato Sauce** (see recipe, page 65)
1 lb (500 g) orecchiette pasta
6 oz (185 g) mozzarella cheese, grated
½ cup (125) freshly grated Pecorino Romano cheese

Tear up the bread and process in a food processor until finely crumbled.
In a large bowl, combine the bread crumbs with the milk and stir to combine.
Set the mixture aside until the crumbs have absorbed the milk, then add the rest of the meatball ingredients; form into small meatballs, about ½-inch (12-mm) in diameter.

In a large heavy pot or Dutch oven, add half of the oil and cook the meatballs in batches over medium heat. Transfer to a bowl and set aside.
Pour out the grease and add the Casa Marinara or Casa Tomato Sauce and bring to a simmer.
Add the meatballs and ½ cup (125) of water; simmer for 30 minutes.

Preheat oven to 375 F (190 C) degrees.

An hour before serving, boil the pasta in salted water for just 5 minutes.
The pasta will continue to cook in the oven.
Drain well and pour the pasta into the pot with the tomato sauce and meatballs.
Gently mix to combine, then pour the mixture into a rectangular baking dish.

Top with grated mozzarella and then with grated Pecorino cheese.

Bake for 25 to 30 minutes, until hot and bubbly.
Loosely cover with aluminum foil if cheese browns too quickly.

Serves 6 to 8

Casazza Lasagne with Beef & Sausage Ragu

This is always a favorite when entertaining a large group of people. You can double the recipe to make two for a crowd (24 slices) or cut the recipe in half (6 slices). It freezes well if you want to make it several days ahead. Just remember to let it thaw for about an hour on the counter before baking, and let it bake a few minutes longer. Lasagna is singular and lasagne is plural.

Beef & Sausage Ragu

2 (28 oz/796 ml) cans whole peeled Italian tomatoes

2 T (30 ml) extra-light olive oil or grape seed oil

1 lb (500 g) mild or hot Italian sausage, casings removed

1 lb (500 g) lean ground beef

1 medium yellow onion, diced

4 cloves garlic, pushed through a garlic press or minced

2 cups (500 ml) canned tomato sauce

1 (6 oz /185 g) can tomato paste

1 cup (250 ml) water

½ cup (125 ml) dry red wine

2 t (10 ml) freeze-dried or chopped fresh basil

1 t (5 ml) freeze-dried or chopped fresh oregano

3 T (45 ml) chopped Italian parsley

1 T (15 ml) granulated sugar (optional)

Salt and freshly ground black pepper

Ricotta Mixture
1 lb (500 g) whole-milk ricotta cheese or optional homemade (recipe follows)
¼ cup (60 ml) minced Italian parsley
¼ t (1 ml) ground nutmeg
½ cup (125 ml) freshly grated Parmigiano-Reggiano cheese
1 large egg, beaten

1 (12 oz/375 g) ball whole-milk mozzarella cheese, sliced
1 lb (500 g) fresh or no-boil lasagne sheets

Pour tomatoes into a large bowl and hand-crush them, removing the hard center cores.
Alternatively, use an immersion blender to chop the tomatoes.

In a large pot or Dutch oven over medium-high heat, add the oil and brown the sausage while breaking up with a wooden spoon. Add the beef, onion, and garlic, and cook another 5 minutes.
Add the crushed tomatoes, tomato sauce, tomato paste, water, wine, herbs, and sugar.
Season to taste with salt and pepper. Partially cover and let simmer 1 ½ hours.

Preheat oven to 375 F (190 C) degrees.
In a medium bowl, mix together the ricotta cheese, parsley, nutmeg, Parmigiano cheese, and egg.

Pour 2 ladles (about 1 ½ cups/375 ml) of the sauce in the bottom of a lasagne pan.
Cover with 5 to 6 overlapping lasagne sheets, then spread half of the ricotta mixture on top and then a layer of the mozzarella cheese. Cover with more sauce and some Parmigiano cheese.
Repeat the layers, ending with a top of Parmigiano.
Cover with aluminum foil that has been sprayed with cooking oil and bake for 30 minutes.
Remove foil and bake another 20 minutes, until cheese is golden brown.
Remove from oven and let cool for 10 minutes before cutting.
Garnish with extra grated Parmigiano cheese and chopped parsley. Serve with a green salad.

Homemade Ricotta Cheese
6 cups (1.5 litres) whole milk
3 T (45 ml) fresh lemon juice
½ t (2 ml) salt

In a heavy, large saucepan, bring milk to a low simmer, just below boiling.
Remove from heat and add the lemon juice and salt and gently stir for one minute.
You will see curds forming. Cover with a lid or tea towel and leave undisturbed for 2 to 3 hours.

Line a colander with 4 layers of cheesecloth; set inside a larger pan. Using a skimmer or slotted spoon, scoop curds from pan and transfer to cheesecloth-lined colander. Let drain 1 hour.

Lift the 4 corners of the cheesecloth and twist cloth to squeeze out most of the liquid.
Transfer curds to a medium bowl, discarding the liquid. Cover and chill until cold, about 3 hours.
Can be made up to 5 days ahead and kept in the refrigerator.

Casazza Lasagne al Forno

Unlike most lasagne recipes, this version is made without ricotta cheese. I bake it in a rectangular baking pan that is 7 by 13 inches (18 by 33 cm), which is smaller than the usual lasagne pan, then cut it into 8 slices. Make the ragu the day before and all you will have to do is assemble and bake the lasagne. You can also partially bake it the day before and finish baking the next day.

2 (28 oz/796 ml) cans whole peeled Italian tomatoes
3 T (45 ml) extra-light olive oil or grape seed oil, divided
1 large onion, diced
4 cloves garlic, pushed through a garlic press or minced
1 ½ lbs (750 g) lean ground beef
1 lb (500 g) ground pork
6 oz (185 g) pancetta, finely diced (optional)
1 (6 oz/185 g) can tomato paste
½ cup (125 ml) red wine
Salt and freshly ground black pepper
1 T (15 ml) chopped fresh basil

8 oz (250 g) mozzarella cheese, grated
2 T (30 ml) freshly grated Parmigiano-Reggiano cheese
1 lb (500 g) fresh or no-boil lasagne sheets

Pour tomatoes into a large bowl and hand-crush them, removing the hard center cores. Alternatively, use an immersion blender to chop the tomatoes. Set aside.

In a large skillet, heat one tablespoon of oil over medium heat.
Add the onion and sauté 10 minutes. Add the garlic and cook another minute. Spoon this mixture into a large pot or Dutch oven.
Add another tablespoon of the oil to the skillet and cook the beef until well browned, breaking up meat with a wooden spoon. Spoon into the pot or Dutch oven.
Add the last tablespoon of oil to the skillet and brown the pork and pancetta. Spoon into the pot or Dutch oven.
Add the chopped tomatoes, tomato paste, and wine to the pot and season to taste with salt and pepper. Bring to a simmer, reduce heat to low, partially cover and simmer for 2 hours, stirring occasionally.

Add the basil 15 minutes before sauce is done.

Besciamella (Bechamel)
6 T (90 ml) unsalted butter
6 T (90 ml) flour
4 cups (1 litre) whole milk
2 t (10 ml) kosher or sea salt
½ t (2 ml) grated nutmeg

In a medium saucepan over medium heat, melt butter until foaming; add flour and cook, whisking constantly for 2 minutes. Do not brown.
Gradually whisk in milk. Increase heat to medium-high and bring quickly to a boil, while whisking constantly. Add salt and nutmeg, reduce the heat to the lowest setting, and simmer 2 minutes. Turn off heat and set aside.

Preheat oven to 375 F (190 C) degrees.

Spread a thin layer of ragu (meat sauce) in bottom of baking pan.
Cover with a ladle of the besciamella sauce, one quarter of the mozzarella, a sprinkling of grated Parmigiano cheese, and a layer of lasagne noodles.
Repeat 3 more times, finishing with a top layer of besciamella and a generous coating of grated cheese.
Cover with aluminum foil that has been sprayed with cooking oil and bake for 30 minutes.
Remove foil and bake another 20 minutes, until cheese is golden brown.

Remove from oven and let cool for 10 minutes before cutting.
Garnish with extra grated Parmigiano cheese and chopped parsley. Serve with a green salad.

Serves 8

Casazza Penne alla Bolognese

The first time I had Bolognese sauce was in Italy back in 1969. I had it again in a restaurant located near Dupont Circle in Washington, D.C. It was only on their "Primi Piatti" (first dishes) menu. I worked on duplicating this recipe for 20 years. A lot of recipes for Bolognese sauce call for a mixture of ground beef, pork, and veal but I prefer just beef and pork. Penne translates to "quills" or "pens." You will find penne pasta in two forms, *lisce* (smooth) or *rigate* (furrowed).

As an option, you can substitute ½ pound (250 grams) of ground veal for ½ pound (250 grams) of the ground beef.

Soffritto
2 medium carrots, peeled and cut into chunks
1 large yellow onion, chopped
4 stalks celery, chopped
4 cloves garlic
2 T (30 ml) extra-light olive oil or grape seed oil

In a food processor fitted with the steel blade, process the carrots, onion, celery, and garlic until finely minced.

In a large pot or Dutch oven, add the oil and cook the vegetable mixture over medium-low heat for 10 minutes. Spoon mixture into a large bowl and set aside.

Meat Sauce
¼ lb (125 g) pancetta, diced
2 T (30 ml) extra-light olive oil or grape seed oil
2 lbs (1 kg) lean ground beef
½ lb (250 g) ground pork
4 cups (1 litre) chicken stock
½ cup (250 ml) dry white wine
1 (13 oz/369 ml) can tomato paste

4 T (60 ml) butter
1 cup (250 ml) milk or half-and-half (half cream)
1 t (5 ml) minced fresh sage
1 t (5 ml) freeze-dried or chopped fresh oregano
2 t (10 ml) freeze-dried or chopped fresh basil
¼ t (1 ml) nutmeg
½ cup (125 ml) freshly grated Parmigiano-Reggiano cheese
Salt and freshly ground black pepper
½ t (2 ml) red pepper flakes
2 T (30 ml) chopped fresh basil, for garnish

1 lb (500 g) penne pasta

In the same large pot or Dutch oven over medium heat, cook the pancetta until golden.
Add 1 tablespoon (15 ml) of oil and half of the ground beef and brown until crumbly, about 10 minutes.
As the meat cooks, break up any chunks with a wooden spoon into small pieces (this is very important). Spoon into the large bowl with the soffritto. Add the other tablespoon (15 ml) of oil and repeat with the rest of the beef and then the pork.

When all of the meat is browned, return it to the pot and add the chicken stock, wine, and tomato paste. Simmer very gently, partially covered, for 2 hours.

Add the butter and the rest of the ingredients and simmer gently for another 15 minutes.

Meanwhile boil penne in salted water for about 8 to 9 minutes, until al dente. Drain and pour penne back into the empty pot.

Mix some of the sauce with the cooked penne and sprinkle with a few chopped basil leaves.
Serve with extra grated Parmigiano cheese. You will have extra sauce left over for another meal.

Serves 4

Chicken

"Pollo"

Chicken Cacciatore with Polenta

Pollo alla Cacciatora con Polenta

This hearty dish was introduced to me by my mother-in-law, Marie Noviello (Novello) Casazza. *Pollo alla cacciatora* in Italy actually means "chicken of the hunter's wife." Cacciatore means "hunter." Chicken cacciatore, as it is called in North America, is a standard of Italian-American home cooking. It is a little similar to coq au vin in French cuisine.

2 (28 oz/796 ml) cans whole peeled Italian tomatoes
¼ cup (60 ml) extra-light olive oil or grape seed oil
2 T (30 ml) unsalted butter
1 whole chicken, cut into 8 pieces, bones and skin left intact
1 ½ cups (375 ml) white or cremini mushrooms, wiped clean, trimmed and sliced
2 medium onions, cut in half and sliced
4 cloves garlic, minced
1 t (5 ml) red pepper flakes
½ cup (125 ml) dry red wine
3 T (45 ml) tomato paste
1 t (5 ml) freeze-dried or chopped fresh oregano
2 bay leaves
Salt and freshly ground black pepper
1 T (15 ml) chopped fresh basil
Freshly grated Parmigianno-Reggiano cheese

Pour tomatoes into a large bowl and hand-crush them, removing the hard center cores. Alternatively, use an immersion blender to chop the tomatoes.

Heat oil and butter in a large heavy pot or Dutch oven over medium-high heat. Season the chicken pieces with salt and pepper and brown them on both sides in two batches. Transfer to a platter and set aside.

Add the mushrooms and onions; cook for 5 minutes. Add the garlic and red pepper flakes and cook another minute.

Add the wine, crushed tomatoes, tomato paste, oregano, and bay leaves. Season to taste with salt and pepper. Stir to combine and bring to a boil, then lower the heat and simmer 15 minutes.

Stir in the reserved chicken, cover and slowly simmer for 30 minutes, or until chicken is tender but not falling off the bones. While the chicken is cooking, make the polenta.

Polenta
4 cups (1 litre) water
4 cups (1 litre) chicken stock
2 t (10 ml) sea salt
2 cups (500 ml) polenta or coarse yellow cornmeal
3 T (45 ml) unsalted butter
¼ cup (60 ml) freshly grated Parmigiano-Reggiano cheese
Salt and freshly ground black pepper

In a large saucepan, bring the water and chicken stock to a boil, then add the sea salt.

Add the polenta to the saucepan in a gentle stream, whisking as you pour. Reduce the heat and let the polenta simmer, whisking constantly for about one minute. Reduce heat to the lowest setting and let simmer for about 20 minutes, stirring often to prevent it from sticking. Remove from stove, add the butter and grated Parmigiano cheese. Season to taste with salt and pepper. Set aside to keep warm.

To Serve
Add the fresh basil to the sauce. Spoon some polenta on plates, place 1 to 2 pieces of chicken on top and spoon on some sauce. Serve with grated Parmigiano cheese at the table.

Serves 4 to 6

Italian Sausage Chicken Roll-Ups
Involtini di Pollo Salsiccia

This dish is easy to do for company because you can make the chicken bundles early in the morning or the day before and finish them up in about 30 minutes, after your company arrives. Serve with roasted potatoes or risotto and a salad. Marsala wine, chicken stock and butter make a wonderful sauce. *Molto buono!*

1 bag (10 oz/300 g) fresh baby spinach, rinsed and drained in a colander
2 hot or mild Italian sausages, about 4 oz (125 g)
¼ cup (60 ml) dry white wine
3 T (45 ml) extra-light olive oil or grape seed oil, divided
2 medium shallots, diced
1 clove garlic, minced
½ cup (125 ml) grated Parmigiano-Reggiano cheese
Salt and freshly ground black pepper
4 boneless, skinless chicken breast halves
¼ cup (60 ml) flour, for dredging

Pour about ¼ cup (60 ml) water into a large skillet, add the spinach, cover, and steam until wilted. This takes a couple of minutes.
Transfer to a bowl using tongs, let cool and discard any liquid in skillet.

Remove sausages from casings and place in a bowl, add the wine, and crush with your hands.

Using the same skillet, add 1 tablespoon (15 ml) of the oil and sauté the shallots over medium heat for 5 minutes. Add the garlic and continue to sauté another minute.
Add the crushed sausage to the skillet and continue to cook until sausage is no longer pink, about 10 minutes. Transfer to a bowl and set aside.

When spinach is cool, squeeze out excess liquid, chop, and place in the bowl with the sausage mixture.
Stir in the grated Parmigiano cheese, season with salt and pepper, and mix well.

Cut each chicken breast almost in half, lengthwise (butterfly).
Spread the breasts open and gently pound each between layers of plastic wrap to ¼-inch (6-mm) thickness, trying not to make holes.

Place 2 tablespoons (30 ml) of the filling in the center of each breast and roll up the sides, then roll up the ends tightly to enclose the filling. Secure with two toothpicks.
Place breasts on a platter, cover, and refrigerate until well chilled, up to 24 hours.

Put the flour in a small bowl and season with salt and pepper.
Dredge the chicken bundles in the flour, shaking off any excess.

In a large skillet, heat the last 2 tablespoons (30 ml) of oil over medium heat.
Brown the chicken for a total of about 20 minutes, turning as needed to brown evenly.
Cover with a lid and cook another 10 minutes to ensure thorough cooking.
Check with an instant-read thermometer for an internal temperature of 165 F (74 C) degrees.
Transfer chicken to a baking sheet and keep warm in a 225 F (110 C) degree oven while making the sauce.

Sauce
½ cup (125 ml) Marsala wine
½ cup (125 ml) chicken stock
3 T (45 ml) unsalted butter
Salt and freshly ground black pepper

Add the Marsala to the skillet and stir to deglaze the pan.
Add the chicken stock and reduce for a couple of minutes.
Add the butter and simmer to let sauce become creamy for another minute.
Season to taste with salt and pepper.

Remove toothpicks from chicken and cut in half diagonally. Pour sauce over and serve.

Serves 4

Rosemary Chicken Roll-Ups
Involtini di Pollo Rosmarino

This dish is the Italian version of chicken cordon bleu but even more delicious . . . *piu delizioso*. You can prepare the chicken the morning before you roast it; then cover and refrigerate it until dinnertime. Roast some potatoes along with the chicken in a separate pan, then add a vegetable or salad and serve this for company. *Buon appetito!*

2 boneless, skinless chicken breast halves
4 thin slices Prosciutto di Parma
4 slices Fontina cheese, at room temperature (for ease in rolling)
2 t (10 ml) chopped fresh rosemary leaves
Salt and freshly ground black pepper
1 cup (250 ml) chicken stock
2 large cloves garlic, cut in half
1 T (15 ml) extra-light olive oil or grape seed oil
½ cup (125 ml) white wine
3 T (45 ml) unsalted butter
2 sprigs rosemary, for garnish

Cut each chicken breast almost in half, lengthwise (butterfly).
Spread the breasts open and gently pound each between layers of plastic wrap to ¼-inch (6-mm) thickness, trying not to make holes.

Layer each chicken breast with 2 slices of prosciutto, 2 slices of Fontina, and a sprinkling of rosemary; season with salt and pepper.
Starting from the long side, fold in the uneven sides slightly and then tightly roll each breast to enclose the filling. Secure with two toothpicks.

Place rolled-up chicken into a bowl or dish and pour the chicken stock over it. Toss in the garlic halves.

Cover and refrigerate until well chilled, up to 24 hours.

Preheat oven to 400 F (200 C) degrees.

Remove chicken from refrigerator, pat it dry, and heat the oil in a cast-iron or ovenproof skillet.
Place chicken in skillet and brown on one side.
Remove from heat and turn the chicken over (brown side on top).

Pour the marinade into the pan. Place in oven and bake for 35 to 40 minutes, uncovered.
Check with an instant-read thermometer for temperature of chicken to 165 F (74 C) degrees.

When done, remove from oven and place chicken on a platter. Remove toothpicks.
Place skillet on top of stove and add the wine.
Bring to a low boil for 1 minute while stirring with a wooden spoon.
Add the butter and stir until melted.

Remove garlic pieces and drizzle sauce over chicken. You can pour the sauce through a strainer, if you want a smoother sauce.

Place a couple sprigs of rosemary on top and serve with roasted potatoes or risotto.

Serves 2

Grilled Spatchcock Lemon-Herb Chicken

Pollo Grigliato al Limone ed Erbe Aromatiche

To spatchcock a chicken you simply remove the backbone with kitchen shears and tuck the drumsticks into slits that you make with a paring knife at the bottom of the breasts. This method reduces the grilling time and ensures more even cooking. In the past I rinsed my chickens before cooking but now research has recommended that you don't, because the water from your kitchen faucet could spread any bacteria from the chicken all over the sink, counter, and you. Cooking the chicken kills any potentially harmful bacteria. It is more important to wash your hands and work area with soap and water after handling raw chicken.

1 (2 to 2 ½ lb/1 to 1.5 kg) whole roasting chicken

Lemon-Herb Sauce
½ cup (125 ml) extra-light olive oil or grape seed oil
6 cloves garlic, pushed through a garlic press or minced
2 T (30 ml) lemon zest
¾ cup (175 ml) fresh lemon juice, about 6 lemons
½ t (2 ml) red pepper flakes
2 T (30 ml) fresh thyme leaves
2 T (30 ml) freeze-dried or chopped fresh oregano
2 T (30 ml) chopped fresh rosemary
Salt and freshly ground black pepper

In a small saucepan, combine the oil and garlic and bring to a simmer for 2 minutes.
Turn off heat and add the lemon zest, lemon juice, red pepper flakes, thyme, oregano, rosemary, and season to taste with salt and pepper; set aside to cool.

Place chicken, breast side down, on a plastic cutting board used for raw meats only.
Cut out the backbone with kitchen shears and cut off any excess fat that you can see.
You can place the backbone in a plastic baggie and freeze it for making stock later.
Flip chicken back over. Using the heel of both hands, flatten breastbone and tuck wing tips under.
To keep the chicken from falling apart (and making it easier to flip over on the grill), cut two holes at the bottom of the breasts on each side and slip the knobby ends of the drumsticks though the slits.

Spoon out about ¼ cup (60 ml) of the Lemon-Herb Sauce into a small bowl.

Place chicken in a baking pan that will fit in your refrigerator and pour the Lemon-Herb Sauce from the small bowl over the chicken. Refrigerate 2 to 8 hours.
Thoroughly wash hands and work surface with soap and water.
Pour the remaining Lemon-Herb Sauce into another bowl, cover and refrigerate.

When ready to cook, prepare your grill with hot coals on one side of a barbecue grill. *

Season chicken with salt and pepper and place, breast side down, on the hot side of the grill.
Place a cast-iron skillet on top of the chicken to weigh it down for nice grill marks.
Grill for about 5 minutes.
Remove skillet and carefully flip the chicken over. Move it to the cool side of the grill.
Close top and cook for about 50 minutes. Remove top and grill another 5 minutes.

Chicken is done when breast meat registers 165 F (74 C) degrees with an instant-read thermometer and juices run clear. Temperature of chicken will continue to rise slightly after removing from the grill. Do not overcook or the breast meat will be dry.

Remove from grill and place on a cutting board; tented with foil and let rest for 10 minutes.

Place the remaining Lemon-Herb Sauce in a small saucepan and heat until hot, but not boiling.
Cut chicken into serving pieces, place on a platter, and pour the sauce over.

Serves 4

* You can also roast the chicken in a 400 F (200 C) degree oven for about 60 to 70 minutes.

Note: Grilling and barbecuing are sometimes used interchangeably, but is incorrect. Grilling is relatively fast and over direct heat and not covered with a top. Barbecuing is over indirect heat with wood, covered, and at a low temperature.

Chicken Breasts Florentine
Petto di Pollo alla Fiorentina

Here is another Italian-American way to serve boneless chicken: on a bed of spinach. This recipe serves two but you can easily double it to serve four. If you don't have dry vermouth, you can substitute white wine—but vermouth is a fortified wine that is aromatized with herbs and spices, and it gives the sauce a wonderful flavor. This is the same dry vermouth that is used in making martinis. Sweet vermouth is used in the Italian drink Negroni, and both are used in the classic American drink, the Manhattan.

2 boneless, skinless chicken breast halves
½ cup (125 ml) flour, for dredging
Salt and freshly ground black pepper
2 T (30 ml) extra-light olive oil or grape seed oil
2 T (30 ml) unsalted butter, divided

116

Sauce
1 T (15 ml) unsalted butter
2 large shallots, cut in half and sliced
1 clove garlic, thinly sliced
¾ cup (175 ml) dry vermouth
½ cup (125 ml) heavy cream or half-and-half (half cream)
2 T (30 ml) chopped Italian parsley, for garnish

Cut each chicken breast in half, lengthwise.
Gently pound chicken between layers of plastic wrap to ¼-inch (6-mm) thickness.

In a shallow bowl, add the flour and season generously with salt and pepper.
Dredge chicken breasts in flour mixture, shaking off excess.
Heat the oil and 1 tablespoon (15 ml) of butter in a large skillet and fry the chicken until golden brown on both sides, about 4 minutes per side.
Add a splash of the vermouth and cook for another minute.

Remove chicken from pan and set aside.

Using the same skillet, add the second tablespoon (15 ml) of butter and sauté the shallots for about 5 minutes. Add the garlic and cook another minute.
Add the remainder of the vermouth and continue to cook and stir for a couple minutes.
Turn heat down to the lowest setting and add the cream or half-and-half and gently heat for one minute.
Return the chicken to the skillet, cover and gently simmer for another 2 minutes.

Spinach
1 T (15 ml) unsalted butter
1 bag (10 oz/300 g) baby spinach, rinsed and drained in a colander
Salt and freshly ground black pepper

Meanwhile, in another very large skillet, melt the butter and add the spinach, season with salt and pepper, and cook while stirring, until lightly wilted. This takes just a few minutes.

Remove spinach with tongs to a warm platter and place the chicken and shallots on top.
Pour the sauce over and serve.

Serves 2

Chicken Marsala

Pollo al Marsala

This recipe is a classic Italian-American dish made with chicken instead of veal. If using veal, the cooking process is a little shorter, about two minutes on each side. The chicken tastes just as good and is less expensive than veal.

2 boneless, skinless chicken breast halves
½ cup (125 ml) flour
Salt and freshly ground black pepper
3 T (45 ml) extra-light olive oil or grape seed oil
3 T (45 ml) unsalted butter
6 white or cremini mushrooms, wiped clean, trimmed and sliced
1 shallot, cut in half and sliced
1 clove garlic, pushed through a garlic press or minced
½ cup (125 ml) Marsala wine
¼ cup (60 ml) chicken stock

Cut each chicken breast in half, lengthwise.
Gently pound chicken between layers of plastic wrap to ¼-inch (6-mm) thickness.
Put flour into a shallow bowl and season generously with salt and pepper.
Dredge chicken in flour and shake off excess.

In a large skillet, heat 1 tablespoon (15 ml) of the oil and 1 tablespoon (15 ml) of the butter over medium-high heat.
Fry half of the chicken for about 4 minutes on each side until golden brown.

Preheat oven to 225 F (110 C) degrees.

Remove pan from heat. Transfer chicken to a baking sheet and keep warm in the oven.

Carefully wipe out skillet with a paper towel and add another 1 tablespoon (15 ml) of oil and 1 tablespoon (15 ml) of butter. Fry the rest of the chicken. Transfer to the baking sheet and keep warm with the rest of the chicken.

Add the rest of the oil and butter to the skillet and cook the mushrooms for 5 minutes.
Add the sliced shallot and cook another 3 minutes.
Add garlic and continue to cook another minute.
Add Marsala wine and continue to cook for a couple of minutes to reduce and thicken slightly.
Add chicken stock and heat through.

Place chicken on 2 plates and spoon the mushrooms and sauce over.

Serve with roasted potatoes and a salad or green vegetable.

Serves 2

Chicken Cutlets Parmigiana
Cotolette di Pollo alla Parmigiana

I have tasted chicken *parmigiana* in so many Italian restaurants from New York City to Chicago and all the way to Seattle. I use a combination of dry bread crumbs and Japanese panko bread crumbs. Panko bread crumbs are extra crispy and do not absorb much oil or add any additional flavors.

One recipe for **Casa Tomato Sauce** (see page 65)

½ cup (125 ml) flour
Salt and freshly ground black pepper
2 eggs
2 T (30 ml) milk or water
1 cup (250 ml) panko bread crumbs
1 cup (250 ml) dried plain bread crumbs
1 cup (250ml) freshly grated Parmigiano-Reggiano cheese, divided
¼ cup (60 ml) finely chopped Italian parsley
1 t (5 ml) garlic powder
2 boneless, skinless chicken breast halves
4 oz (125 g) mozzarella cheese, sliced
3 T (45 ml) extra-light olive oil or grape seed oil
1 lb (500 g) spaghetti, cooked al dente
Casa Tomato Sauce, kept warm on stove

Put flour in a shallow bowl and season generously with salt and pepper.
Pour eggs in another shallow bowl and whisk with the milk or water.
Put bread crumbs, ¼ cup (60 ml) of the Parmigiano cheese, parsley, and garlic powder in a third shallow bowl.

Cut each chicken breast in half, lengthwise.
Gently pound chicken between layers of plastic wrap to ¼-inch (6-mm) thickness.
Lightly dredge both sides of the chicken in the seasoned flour, then dip in the egg mixture and finally into the bread crumbs.
Set chicken aside on a large platter or baking sheet.

Preheat oven to 375 F (190 C) degrees.

Heat the oil over medium-high heat in a large skillet.
Add the chicken to the skillet, 2 pieces at a time, and fry for about 4 minutes on each side.
Place cutlets on a clean baking sheet while frying the rest.

Place the last 2 cutlets on the baking sheet and spoon a little of the Casa Tomato Sauce on top of each, sprinkle with the rest of the Parmigiano cheese and arrange a slice of mozzarella on top.

Bake in oven for about 5 minutes or until cheese is melted, but not brown.
Serve with a side of spaghetti that has been tossed with more of the Casa Tomato Sauce.

Serves 2 to 4

Chicken Piccata
Piccata di Pollo

Chicken *piccata* is on the menu in most Italian restaurants, and it is so easy to prepare at home. The recipe originated in Italy with veal. Serve this with Risotto alla Milanese (see recipe, page 180).

2 boneless, skinless chicken breasts halves
½ cup (125 ml) flour
Salt and freshly ground black pepper
2 eggs
2 T (30 ml) milk or water
1 ½ cups (375 ml) panko bread crumbs
½ cup (125 ml) plain dry bread crumbs
2 T (30 ml) extra-light olive oil or grape seed oil, divided
3 T (45 ml) unsalted butter
Juice of 1 medium lemon
½ cup (125 ml) chicken stock
¼ cup (60 ml) dry vermouth
¼ cup (60 ml) capers, drained
½ lemon, thinly sliced into circles

Cut each chicken breast in half, lengthwise.
Gently pound chicken between layers of plastic wrap to ¼-inch (6-mm) thickness.

In a shallow bowl, add the flour and season generously with salt and pepper.
In another shallow bowl, whisk together the eggs and milk or water.
In a third shallow bowl, mix together the panko and plain dry bread crumbs.

Dredge chicken in flour and shake off excess. Then dip the pieces into the beaten egg mixture and finally into the bread crumb mixture. Set aside on a large platter or baking sheet.

Preheat oven to 225 F (110 C) degrees.

Heat 1 tablespoon (15 ml) oil over medium-high heat in a large skillet.
Add the chicken to the skillet, 2 pieces at a time, and fry for about 4 minutes on each side.
Transfer cutlets to a clean baking sheet and keep warm in the oven.
Fry the other 2 pieces of chicken in 1 tablespoon (15 ml) of oil and then place in the oven with the rest of the cutlets.

Carefully wipe out the skillet with dry paper towels. Over medium heat, melt the butter and then add the lemon juice, chicken stock and vermouth. Season to taste with salt and pepper.
Bring to a low boil and reduce for about 2 minutes.
Turn off heat, add the capers, and stir to combine.

Place 1 or 2 cutlets on individual plates or a platter and spoon on the sauce.
Garnish with a few slices of lemon.

Serves 2 to 4

Chicken Milanese with Tomato Salsa
Cotoletta di Pollo con Salsa di Pomodoro

I had this wonderful crispy chicken dish in a restaurant in Amalfi, Italy. Arugula is also known as rocket in Italy and probably comes from the French word *roquette*. You can also make this with veal, but cook the veal for only 2 minutes on each side. Serve with your favorite Italian wine. *Molto delizioso!*

Fresh Tomato Salsa
2 cups (500 ml) red or multi-colored cherry tomatoes, diced
3 T (45 ml) extra-virgin olive oil
2 t (10 ml) balsamic vinegar
2 cloves garlic, minced
2 T (30 ml) chopped fresh basil
½ t (2 ml) chopped fresh oregano
Salt and freshly ground black pepper

Mix the above ingredients together in a bowl, cover and set aside while making the chicken.

Chicken Cutlets
4 boneless, skinless chicken breast halves
1 cup (250 ml) flour
Salt and freshly ground black pepper
2 eggs
2 T (30 ml) milk or water
2 T (30 ml) freshly grated Parmigiano-Reggiano or Pecorino Romano cheese
1 ½ cups (375 ml) panko bread crumbs
½ cup (125 ml) plain dry bread crumbs
¼ cup (60 ml) extra-light olive oil or grape seed oil, for frying
4 small handfuls arugula, washed and dried (one handful for each plate)
Shaved Parmigiano-Reggiano or Pecorino Romano cheese, for garnish

Cut each chicken breast in half, lengthwise.
Gently pound chicken between layers of plastic wrap to ¼-inch (6-mm) thickness.

In a shallow bowl, add the flour and season generously with salt and pepper.
In another shallow bowl, whisk together the eggs with the milk or water and cheese.
In a third shallow bowl, mix together the panko and plain dry bread crumbs.

Dredge chicken in flour and shake off excess. Then dip the pieces into the beaten egg mixture and finally into the bread crumb mixture.
Set aside on a platter or baking sheet while breading the other pieces.

Preheat oven to 225 F (110 C) degrees.

Pour 2 tablespoons (30 ml) of oil into a large skillet and heat over medium-high heat.
Cook cutlets in batches for about 4 minutes on each side then place on a baking sheet and keep warm in the oven while cooking the rest.
Wipe out the skillet with paper towels before cooking the remaining cutlets.

Spoon some of the tomato salsa on the bottom of each plate, place two chicken cutlets on top, and then top with some arugula. Finish up with some shavings of cheese.

Serves 4

Chicken Milanese with Lemon
Pollo alla Milanese con Limone

Chicken Milanese is a traditional Italian dish. It can also be made with veal. The panko bread crumbs make the chicken very crisp without adding any additional flavors. Panko is usually sold where you find flour or dry bread crumbs. You can omit the Lemon-Butter sauce if desired and just serve the chicken with a couple of lemon slices.

2 boneless, skinless chicken breast halves
½ cup (125 ml) flour
Salt and freshly ground black pepper
1 egg
1 T (15 ml) milk or water
1 cup (250 ml) panko bread crumbs
½ cup (125 ml) plain dry bread crumbs
2 T (30 ml) extra-light olive oil or grape seed oil

Cut each chicken breast in half, lengthwise.
Gently pound chicken between layers of plastic wrap to ¼-inch (6-mm) thickness.

In a shallow bowl, add the flour and season generously with salt and pepper.
In another shallow bowl, whisk together the egg with the milk or water.
In a third shallow bowl, mix together the panko and plain dry bread crumbs.

Dredge chicken in flour and shake off excess. Then dip the pieces into the beaten egg mixture and finally into the bread crumb mixture.
Set aside on a platter or baking sheet while breading the other pieces.

Preheat oven to 225 F (110 C).

Heat the oil in a large non-stick skillet over medium-high heat. Add the chicken breasts and cook about 4 minutes on each side, until golden brown.
Transfer chicken to a baking sheet and keep warm in the oven while making the sauce.

Lemon-Butter Sauce
3 T (45 ml) unsalted butter
1 lemon (cut off 2 circles and cut circles in half, save the rest for juice)
½ cup (125 ml) dry white wine
2 T (30 ml) chopped Italian parsley, for garnish

Wipe out the skillet with a paper towel and melt 1 tablespoon (15 ml) of the butter.
Add the juice of the lemon and the wine. Season to taste with salt and pepper.
Bring to a boil and let reduce by half, about 2 minutes.
Turn off heat and add the other 2 tablespoons (30 ml) of the butter and swirl to combine.

Place 2 chicken cutlets on each plate and spoon some of the sauce over.
Garnish with a small sprinkling of parsley and a couple slices of lemon.

Serves 2

Meats

"Carni"

Italian Sausages with Peppers & Onions
Salsicce con Peperoni e Cipolle

Get the best Italian sausages you can find. If you have any leftovers, put the sausages and peppers on a roll with spicy mustard or pair them with tomato sauce and cheese for an Italian Sausage Grinder (see recipe, page 138).

3 T (45 ml) extra-light olive oil or grape seed oil, divided
8 (about 1 ½ lbs/750 g) good-quality Italian sausages, hot or sweet
6 bell peppers, various colors, seeded and sliced
2 large yellow onions, cut in half and sliced
2 cloves garlic, minced
1 t (5 ml) freeze-dried or chopped fresh oregano
Salt and freshly ground black pepper

Heat 1 tablespoon (15 ml) of the oil in a large skillet over medium heat.
Add the sausages and fry, turning several times, for about 20 minutes.
Transfer to a cutting board; pour the grease from the skillet and discard.
Let skillet cool and wipe out with paper towels, or use a clean skillet.

Heat the other 2 tablespoons (30 ml) of oil over medium heat, add the peppers and onions, and cook for another 8 to 10 minutes.

Slice the sausages diagonally into 3 or 4 pieces each and return to skillet with the peppers and onions.
Lower heat and add the garlic and oregano; season to taste with salt and pepper, and cook another 5 minutes.

Serve with a side of Polenta (see recipe, page 109)

Serves 4 to 6

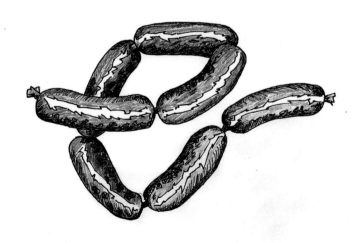

Roasted Pork Tenderloin Wrapped In Bacon

Filetto di Maiale Arrosto con Pancetta

Pork tenderloin can be dry and tasteless, but you can add a variety of sauces to add flavor to the pork. This is a delicious and different way to roast it, wrapped in bacon and sprinkled with herbs. It is quick, easy, incredibly delicious—and your whole house will smell wonderful while it roasts. Pork tenderloins often come two in a pack and are enough to serve four. Of course, you can always roast one and freeze the other.

2 pork tenderloins, about 1 ¼ lbs (625 g) each
¼ cup (60 ml) brown sugar
¼ cup (60 ml) Dijon mustard
1 t (5 ml) salt
½ t (2 ml) freshly ground black pepper
2 T (30 ml) chopped fresh rosemary
2 T (30 ml) chopped Italian parsley
2 T (30 ml) fresh thyme leaves
8 bacon slices, cut in half

Preheat oven to 450 F (230 C) degrees.

Line a baking sheet with aluminum foil. This is very important so you don't ruin your pan.

Slice off and remove the tough silver skin from the tenderloins, leaving any visible fat in place.
In a small bowl, stir together the sugar, mustard, salt, pepper, and herbs.
Spoon the sugar-mustard sauce on the tenderloins, smoothing it all over.

Fold under the small end of each tenderloin, then wrap the bacon halves around tops, tucking the ends of the bacon underneath.

Place in oven and roast for about 20 to 25 minutes, or until the internal temperature reaches 140 F (60 C) degrees.

Let rest 5 minutes and slice.

Serve with roasted potatoes and a green vegetable or salad.

One tenderloin serves 2 to 3
Two tenderloins serves 4 to 6

Pork Chops with Port Wine
Maiale con Vino Porto

Trim the meat away from the end of each pork chop (called "frenching") for a prettier presentation, and save the trimmings for the sauce. You can also have your butcher do this for you. The port wine sauce adds a wonderful flavor to the pork chops.

2 T (30 ml) extra-light olive oil or grape seed oil, divided
Pork chop trimmings
1 shallot, thinly sliced
1 T (15 ml) fresh rosemary leaves
1 clove garlic, pushed through a garlic press or minced
½ cup (125 ml) port
½ cup (125 ml) beef broth
Salt and freshly ground black pepper
1 T (15 ml) unsalted butter
2 bone-in pork chops, 1-inch (2.5-cm) thick

Heat 1 tablespoon of the oil in a heavy cast-iron skillet over medium heat.
Add the pork chop trimmings and cook for 4 to 5 minutes.
Lower the heat and add the shallot and rosemary leaves, and cook for about 5 minutes.
Add the garlic and cook another minute.
Raise the heat to medium-high and carefully add the port. Cook, stirring, for 2 minutes.
Add the beef broth and simmer for a few minutes.
Season to taste with salt and pepper.
Turn off heat and swirl in the butter.
Pour through a strainer into a small saucepan and keep warm while cooking the pork chops.

Season the chops with salt and pepper.

Wipe out the same cast-iron skillet and add the other 1 tablespoon (15 ml) of oil.
Brown the chops on each side for 5 minutes. Place a lid on the skillet and cook over low heat until pork chops have an internal temperature of 140 F (60 C) degrees, about 10 minutes.
Turn the chops over halfway through the cooking time.

Transfer chops to warm plates and drizzle on some of the warm port sauce.

Serves 2

Italian Grinder

Whether you call it a sub, hoagie, hero, or grinder, this is a quintessential Italian-American sandwich.

1 loaf crusty Italian bread, cut into 2 (6-inch/15-cm) pieces
Mayonnaise
Capicola or other Italian ham, sliced
Pepperoni, sliced
Genoa salami, sliced
Provolone cheese, sliced
Shredded lettuce
Onion slices
Tomato slices
Pepperoncini peppers, stems removed and sliced

Extra-virgin olive oil
Red wine vinegar
Garlic powder
Freeze-dried or chopped fresh oregano
Red pepper flakes
Salt and freshly ground black pepper

Cut the bread in half to get two pieces, each about 6-inches (15-cm) long. Then slice the pieces lengthwise to make sandwich rolls.
Spread a little mayonnaise on each side of the bread.

Layer the bottom half with a slice of the ham, pepperoni, salami, and provolone.
Place under the broiler for a minute or two, just to melt the cheese.

Add the lettuce, onion slices, tomato slices, and pepperoncini.
Drizzle with a little extra-virgin olive oil and red wine vinegar.

Sprinkle with a little garlic powder, oregano, and red pepper flakes.
Season to taste with salt and pepper.

Place the top half of bread on and serve.

Serves 2

Italian Sausage Grinder

This is another grinder made with Italian sausages. You can also make it with meatballs. All you need for the perfect meal is a green salad and a glass of *vino rosso*.

Extra-light olive oil or grape seed oil
4 mild or hot Italian sausages
1 medium onion, cut in half and sliced
1 large green bell pepper, seeded and sliced

1 (28 oz/796 ml) can whole peeled Italian tomatoes
½ medium onion, diced
½ t (2 ml) red pepper flakes
2 cloves garlic, pushed through a garlic press or minced
2 T (30 ml) tomato paste
1 t (5 ml) freeze-dried or chopped fresh oregano
1 t (5 ml) freeze-dried or chopped fresh basil
½ cup (125 ml) red wine, optional
Salt and freshly ground black pepper
4 hoagie rolls
Provolone and Parmigiano-Reggiano cheeses, for topping

In a Dutch oven or large saucepan, add a little of the oil and brown the sausages on both sides. Transfer to a plate and set aside.

In a skillet, add a little more oil and sauté the onion and bell pepper slices until soft, about 10 to 12 minutes. Set aside and keep warm on stove.

Meanwhile pour the tomatoes in a bowl and hand-crush them. Alternatively, use an immersion blender to coarsely chop the tomatoes.

Drain off most of the grease from the Dutch oven or saucepan and add a little more oil.
Sauté the diced onion for 5 minutes, then add the red pepper flakes and garlic; sauté another minute. Add the crushed tomatoes, tomato paste, oregano, basil, and wine.
Season to taste with salt and pepper.
Simmer for 15 minutes; add the browned sausages and simmer another 30 minutes.

Open the hoagie rolls and place them under the broiler for 2 to 3 minutes, until golden brown.

Place one sausage on each of the 4 toasted rolls.
Add a little tomato sauce and top with some of the sliced onions and peppers.
Lay on a slice of provolone cheese and sprinkle with Parmigiano.
Place under the broiler just until the cheese melts but doesn't burn, about 1 to 2 minutes.

Serves 4

Brooklyn Pizzaiola Steak Sandwich

Philadelphia has its Philly cheese steak sandwich and Brooklyn has its *pizzaiola* steak sandwich. They are similar but the pizzaiola has three cheeses and one extra ingredient—tomato sauce "gravy." This sandwich is truly a meal in itself. *Panino Grande!*

2 (6 oz/185 g) boneless New York strip steaks or any steaks of your choice
1 T (15 ml) unsalted butter
2 T (30 ml) extra-light olive oil
1 (14 oz/398 ml) can whole peeled Italian tomatoes
1 small yellow onion, diced
3 cloves garlic, pushed through a garlic press or finely minced
½ t (2 ml) red pepper flakes
1 (28 oz/796 ml) can tomato sauce
1 T (15 ml) tomato paste
1 t (5 ml) freeze-dried or chopped fresh basil
1 cup (250 ml) water
Salt and freshly ground black pepper
1 medium yellow onion, cut in half and sliced
2 bell peppers, sliced, any color you prefer
1 large loaf crusty Italian bread, cut into four (6-inch/15-cm) pieces
Parmigiano-Reggiano cheese, grated
4 slices provolone cheese
4 slices mozzarella cheese

Slice both steaks in half lengthwise to make 4 thin pieces.
Place one of the pieces between layers of plastic wrap and pound it until it is about ¼-inch (6-mm) thick. Repeat with the other 3 pieces.

In a large pan over medium-high heat, melt the butter with the oil and brown each piece of beef about 5 minutes on each side. Remove and set aside.

Meanwhile pour the tomatoes in a bowl and hand-crush them. Alternatively, use an immersion blender to coarsely chop the tomatoes.

Add the onion to the large pan and sauté for 10 minutes.
Add the garlic, red pepper flakes, crushed tomatoes, tomato sauce, tomato paste, basil, and water; season to taste with salt and pepper.
Simmer for 15 minutes.
Add the beef to the pan and cover completely with sauce. Simmer on very low heat, covered, for 2 hours. The sauce will be thick.

Meanwhile, in a skillet, add a little oil and sauté the sliced onion and bell peppers until soft, about 15 minutes; set aside.

To make the sandwiches:
Slice bread in half lengthwise and brush with some olive oil.
Place under a broiler for a couple of minutes, until light golden.
Place steak slices on bottom halves of the rolls, spoon on some gravy, add some of the onions and bell peppers, and sprinkle with some Parmigiano cheese.
Top with the provolone.
Place the mozzarella cheese on the top half of bread.

Keep sandwich open and place under the broiler again, broiling until the cheeses are melted but not browned, about 1 to 2 minutes.
Cut each sandwich in half and serve.

Serves 4

Big Mamma's Sunday Braciole with Gravy

Braciole is a traditional Sunday Italian-American dinner. It's made even better by adding a little pasta or polenta on the side. The rolled beef simmers slowly on the stove for several hours. While the amazing aroma of this cooking fills the house, listen to a couple of Puccini operas, Luciano Pavarotti, or Enrico Caruso. You can prepare the steak the day before and refrigerate it. For added flavor, add a few Italian sausages to the gravy. Brown them before you brown the steaks and simmer together.

Filling

½ cup (125 ml) pine nuts (pignoli)
¼ cup (60 ml) extra-light olive oil or grape seed oil
½ cup (125 ml) homemade bread crumbs or plain dry bread crumbs
¼ cup (60 ml) freshly grated Parmigiano-Reggiano or Grana Padano cheese
¼ cup (60 ml) freshly grated Pecorino Romano cheese
¼ cup (60 ml) chopped Italian parsley
2 cloves garlic, minced
Salt and freshly ground black pepper

Toast pine nuts in a dry skillet until golden. When nuts are cool, finely chop and add to a medium bowl. Add the rest of the above ingredients to the bowl and mix together.

1 (1 ½ lb/750g) boneless beef top round steak or boneless beef chuck flat-iron steak
5 to 6 thin slices Prosciutto di Parma

With a very sharp knife, butterfly the steak and open it up.

Lay the prosciutto across the steak, covering the surface.

Spread the filling on top of the prosciutto, leaving a border around all of the sides.

Carefully roll up into a long roll and secure with several pieces of cotton butcher's twine.

Trim off long ends of twine.

Cut the completed roll in half, if necessary, to fit into your pot.

Tomato Sauce "Gravy"

2 T (30 ml) extra-light olive oil or grape seed oil

4 oz (125 g) pancetta, diced

1 medium onion, diced

2 cloves garlic, pushed through a garlic press or minced

1 cup (250 ml) good-quality red wine

1 (28 oz/796 ml) can whole peeled Italian tomatoes

1 (28 oz/796 ml) can tomato sauce

1 (6 oz/185 g) can tomato paste

1 T (15 ml) freeze-dried or chopped fresh basil

1 cup (250 ml) cold water

Salt and freshly ground black pepper

8 to 10 basil leaves, cut into thin strips (chiffonade), for garnish

In a large heavy pot or Dutch oven over medium-high heat, heat the oil until hot.

Add the rolled steak or steaks to the pan and brown on all sides, then remove and set aside.

Lower heat to medium and add the pancetta; cook until golden.

Add the onion and sauté another 3 minutes.

Add the garlic and sauté another minute.

Add the wine and bring to a low boil, scraping the bottom of the pan with a wooden spoon.

Meanwhile pour the tomatoes in a bowl and hand-crush them. Alternatively, use an immersion blender to coarsely chop the tomatoes.

Add the crushed tomatoes, tomato sauce, tomato paste, and basil. Stir to combine.

Add the water and season to taste with salt and pepper.

Return the steak roll or rolls to the pan, partially cover, and simmer very slowly for 3 to 3 ½ hours. Gently stir occasionally.

Remove the rolled braciole and set aside on a cutting board for 10 minutes.

Remove twine and cut braciole crosswise into thick slices.

Transfer to a warm platter and spoon some gravy over, then sprinkle with basil strips.

Serves 4

Grilled Steaks with Gorgonzola Butter
Bistecche alla Griglia con Burro di Gorgonzola

Butter, butter, what could be better? How about Gorgonzola Butter and Basil Butter (recipes follow).

Gorgonzola Butter

¼ cup (60 ml) unsalted butter, softened to room temperature
2 scallions, minced
2 T (30 ml) crumbled Gorgonzola cheese, room temperature
Salt and freshly ground black pepper

In a bowl, using a fork, smash the soft butter until no lumps appear.
Add the scallions and cheese and season to taste with salt and pepper.
Mix until well combined.

Spoon onto a piece of parchment or wax paper and roll into a log about 6-inches (15-cm) long.
Twist ends and place in the refrigerator to harden.
This can be done a few hours or a couple of days prior to cooking the steaks.

Basil Butter

2 T (30 ml) unsalted butter, softened
1 t (5 ml) minced fresh basil
Salt and freshly ground black pepper

Mix the butter and basil together in a small bowl and season to taste with salt and pepper.
Set aside.

Steaks

2 bone-in or boneless New York steaks, or any steaks of your choice
Salt and freshly ground black pepper
Red wine

Trim excess fat from meat and place on a large plate. Season to taste with salt and pepper on both sides. Drizzle with some red wine and place in refrigerator for 30 minutes.
Take steaks out of the refrigerator, turn over, and let come to room temperature before cooking.

Grill steaks over hot coals for 4 to 6 minutes each side or pan fry in a large cast-iron skillet.
Put the steaks on two plates, add a pat of the Gorgonzola Butter on top of each steak and serve with mashed potatoes with a spoonful of Basil Butter.

Serves 2

Italian Pot Roast

My mother made southern-style pot roast on Sundays, alternating with southern fried chicken. I still remember how delicious and comforting it was, and this recipe has a little more zing to it's . . . because it's Italian! It has garlic, Italian tomatoes, and a surprising ingredient: toasted pine nuts (*pignoli*). Serve this with mashed potatoes and Peas with Pancetta (see recipe, page 182).

1 boneless chuck-eye roast (about 3 lbs/1.5 kg), tied with cotton butcher's twine
Salt and freshly ground black pepper
1 T (15 ml) extra-light olive oil
½ cup (125 ml) pine nuts
1 medium onion, quartered
2 carrots, peeled, each cut into three pieces
2 stalks celery, each cut into three pieces
4 cloves garlic, pushed through a garlic press or minced
1 T (15 ml) tomato paste
2 cups (500 ml) Merlot or other dry red wine
1 (28 oz/796 ml) can whole peeled Italian tomatoes
1 sprig each thyme and rosemary
2 T (30 ml) softened butter mixed with 2 T (30 ml) flour

Pat the roast dry with paper towels and season all over with salt and pepper.

Place a large heavy pot or Dutch oven over medium heat, add the oil, and brown the beef on all sides, including the ends.
While beef is browning, toast the pine nuts in a dry skillet until golden and set aside.
After beef is brown, set aside on a platter.

Reduce heat to medium and add the onion, carrots, and celery; sauté for 5 minutes.
Add the garlic and sauté another 2 minutes.

Preheat oven to 325 F (160 C) degrees.

Add tomato paste to pot and cook another minute.
Add wine and stir with a wooden spoon to loosen the flavorful brown particles.
Pour the can of tomatoes and pignoli nuts into a large bowl and puree a few seconds with an electric immersion blender. You can also do this quickly in a standard blender.
Pour into the pot along with the thyme and rosemary sprigs and return roast to pan.
Raise heat to boil, then cover with a lid and place in oven for 1 ½ hours.
Remove from oven and carefully flip meat over with tongs. Roast covered, another 1 ½ hours.

Transfer beef to a cutting board and tent with aluminum foil to keep warm.
Place pot on stovetop and with a slotted spoon, remove the vegetables and herbs and discard.
Skim off any fat from the surface.
Bring the pot to a boil and add butter-flour mixture; whisk for a couple of minutes until slightly thickened. Pour sauce through a strainer into a smaller saucepan and keep hot.

Remove butcher's twine from meat and carve roast against the grain into ½-¾ inch (12-18 mm) thick slices and place on a warm platter or on individual plates.
Pour a little warm sauce over roast and add the rest to a gravy boat.

Serves 6

Grilled Steak Tagliata
Bistecca alla Griglia Tagliata

This dish was originally from Tuscany, but I have had it in two different restaurants in Positano, Italy. To me, the perfect accompaniment is a plate of crispy French fries. *Tagliata* translates to "cut" in Italian.

1 ½ lbs (750 g) boneless sirloin steak (or any steak of your choice)
2 T (30 ml) chopped fresh rosemary
1 t (5 ml) freeze-dried or chopped fresh oregano
1 clove garlic, pushed through a garlic press or minced
Salt and freshly ground black pepper
3 T (45 ml) extra-light olive oil

Place the above marinade ingredients in a large zippered plastic bag.
Pat steaks dry with paper towels, then place in the bag, squeeze out most of the air and swish around to coat the steak evenly with herbs and oil.

Refrigerate 2 to 4 hours.

148

Vinaigrette
¼ cup (60 ml) fresh lemon juice
½ t (2 ml) Dijon mustard
Salt and freshly ground black pepper
½ cup (125 ml) extra-virgin olive oil

In a medium bowl, whisk together the lemon juice and Dijon mustard; season to taste with salt and pepper.
While whisking, slowly add the olive oil in a stream and continue to whisk until the dressing thickens slightly. Set aside.

1 (10 oz/300 g) bag baby arugula (enough to fill 4 plates)

Balsamic vinegar
Parmigiano-Reggiano cheese, shaved
4 lemon wedges

Grill steak over hot coals for 5 to 8 minutes each side, turning once.
Check with an instant-read thermometer for a temperature of 120 to 125 F (49 to 52 C) degrees for medium rare.
Transfer to a cutting board, cover loosely with aluminum foil, and let rest for 5 to 7 minutes.

While the meat is resting, put the arugula in a bowl and drizzle with some of the vinaigrette.
Toss to coat with dressing and distribute onto 4 individual plates.

Slice the meat thinly across the grain and place the slices over the beds of arugula.
Pour on any accumulated meat juices, sprinkle with a little balsamic vinegar, top with shaved Parmigiano-Reggiano cheese, and add a lemon wedge.

Serves 4

Seafood

"Frutti di Mare"

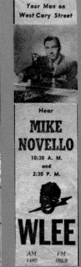

Your Man on
West Cary Street

Hear

MIKE
NOVELLO

10:30 A. M.
and
2:30 P. M.

WLEE

AM   FM
1480   101.9

Fried Squid
Calamari Fritti

Fried calamari is so delicious and crispy if you follow these instructions . . . even better than in a restaurant. Serve the calamari with lemon wedges and Lemon Aioli, for dipping (recipe follows).

Lemon Aioli
½ cup (110 g) mayonnaise
2 t (10 ml) finely grated lemon zest
2 T (30 ml) fresh lemon juice
1 t (5 ml) Dijon mustard
1 small clove garlic, pushed through a garlic press or minced
Sea salt and freshly ground black pepper

In a small bowl, mix together the mayonnaise, lemon zest, juice, mustard, and garlic. Season to taste with salt and pepper. Refrigerate until needed.

Calamari
1 lb (500 g) cleaned squid, with tentacles
1 cup (250 ml) milk
2 T (30 ml) fresh lemon juice
1 to 2 t (5 to 10 ml) hot sauce
¾ cup (175 ml) cornstarch
¾ cup (175 ml) corn flour
¾ cup (175 ml) panko bread crumbs
1 t (5 ml) sea salt
½ t (2 ml) black pepper
½ t (2 ml) garlic powder
2 eggs
2 T (30 ml) water or milk
Peanut oil, for deep frying
Lemon wedges, for serving

If buying whole squid, gently twist and pull head away from the body. With a sharp knife, slice the tentacles from the head, just above the eyes. Take the beak (mouth) out from inside the tentacles. Discard head and beak, and set tentacles aside. Rinse squid tubes under cold water. Pull out and discard the cuttlebone (clear, long, plastic-like skeleton).
Or you can buy squid already cleaned, fresh or frozen, at fishmongers and some supermarkets.

Pour milk in a large bowl and add the lemon juice.
Let sit for 10 minutes, then add the hot sauce and the squid.

In a shallow bowl, add the cornstarch, corn flour, panko bread crumbs, salt, pepper, and garlic powder; mix with a fork.
In another shallow bowl, whisk the eggs with the water or milk.

Preheat oven to 225 F (110 C) degrees.

Using very clean hands, remove a few squid pieces from the milk and dip them into the egg mixture and then dredge them in the dry mixture, making sure they are thoroughly coated.
Place on a baking sheet lined with wax paper or parchment paper.

Heat peanut oil in a deep fryer to 365 F (185 C) degrees and fry squid in batches for only about 2 minutes to a medium golden brown. Do not cook longer or the calamari will be tough.
Keep the first batch warm on a paper towel-lined baking sheet in the oven while frying the second batch.

Season with a little more sea salt and serve with Lemon Aioli and plenty of lemon wedges.

Serves 2 to 4

Seafood in Crazy Water
Frutti di Mare all'Acqua Pazza

Acqua pazza is a term used in Italian cuisine to refer to a recipe for poached seafood.
I used rockfish in this recipe along with clams and mussels. If you live near the southeastern Atlantic Ocean or the Gulf of Mexico, you can get red snapper. If you live near the Pacific Ocean, you get what is called rockfish or Pacific red snapper—they are both a type of bass, but any firm white fish will be great with this recipe.

2 cups (500 ml) whole peeled Italian tomatoes
1 small onion, cut in half and thinly sliced
1 small bulb fennel, thinly sliced (save a few fronds)
2 T (30 ml) extra-light olive oil or grape seed oil
3 cloves garlic, pushed through a garlic press or minced
1 t (5 ml) fresh thyme leaves
1 t (5 ml) chopped fresh oregano
½ t (2 ml) fennel seeds
1 T (15 ml) finely grated lemon zest
Sea salt and freshly ground black pepper

½ cup (125 ml) dry white wine or water
12 cultivated or wild mussels
12 small clams
2 (8 oz/250 g) red snapper or rockfish fillets

Pour tomatoes into a bowl and hand-crush them, removing the hard center cores.
Alternatively, use an immersion blender to chop the tomatoes.

In a large skillet over medium heat, sauté the onion and fennel in the oil until softened, about 10 minutes. Add the garlic and sauté another minute.
Add the thyme, oregano, fennel seeds, lemon zest, and the crushed tomatoes.
Season to taste with salt and pepper.
Bring to a boil, lower heat and simmer, partially covered, for 30 minutes.

While sauce is simmering, scrub mussels and clams with a brush under cold running water.
If using wild mussels, remove beards with a pair of "kitchen only" needle-nose pliers.
Add the wine or water to a medium saucepan and bring to a boil.
Add the mussels and clams, cover, reduce heat and simmer until shells open, about 6 to 7 minutes.
Remove shellfish with a slotted spoon and set aside in a covered bowl, to keep warm.
Discard any shells that failed to open.
Strain the liquid through a fine mesh colander and add to the simmering tomato sauce.

When the tomato sauce is almost done, preheat oven to 475 F (240 C) degrees.

Place fish on a lightly oiled baking sheet, drizzle with a little more oil and season to taste
with salt and pepper. Bake in oven for 10 to 12 minutes.

Place fish on each warm plate or pasta bowl, surround with the shellfish and spoon on some of the sauce.
Add some lemon slices and a few fennel fronds and serve.

Serves 2

Roasted Salmon with Beans & Tomato Salsa

Salmone con Fagioli e Salsa di Pomodoro

This recipe was given to me by my sister, Dotti Vallone. She calls this her "go to" recipe when she wants to make a delicious dinner that is fast and easy. Salmon is such a healthy fish to eat because of its omega-3 fatty acid content. Also salmon accumulates very few heavy metals in its lifetime. I served this with Scalloped Potatoes with Quattro Formaggi (see recipe, page 183).

Salsa
½ medium onion, diced
½ (14 oz/398 ml) can cannellini beans, rinsed and drained
½ cup (125 ml) pitted and chopped Italian black olives
½ cup (125 ml) cherry tomatoes, cut in quarters
2 T (30 ml) chopped fresh basil
2 T (30 ml) chopped Italian parsley
Extra-light olive oil, for sautéing

Salmon
2 (8 oz/250g) wild salmon fillets
Sea salt and freshly ground black pepper
Extra-light olive oil, for roasting
Juice of ½ lemon

Put the diced onion in a small bowl and set aside.
Put the beans, olives and tomatoes in another bowl and set aside.
Put the basil and parsley in a third bowl and set aside.

Preheat oven to 400 F (200 C) degrees.

Remove any bones from salmon with a pair of "kitchen only" needle-nose pliers.
Season salmon to taste with salt and pepper, and drizzle with some olive oil.
Place on a baking sheet, skin side down, and roast for 10 minutes.

While salmon is roasting, sauté the onion in a little olive oil for 2 minutes until slightly softened.
Add the beans, olives, and tomatoes and cook over medium heat while stirring, until heated through, about 3 minutes.

Remove from heat and stir in the basil and parsley.

Remove salmon from oven. Transfer the fillets to individual warmed plates. The skin will remain on the baking sheet when you lift the salmon with a spatula. Squeeze lemon juice on top and serve with the salsa on the side.

Serves 2

Note: Try to find King salmon, also known as Chinook.
    Sockeye, also known as Red, is leaner but is every bit as delicious.

Mussels with Tomatoes, Fennel & Wine

Cozze con Pomodori, Finocchio e Vino

I prefer cultivated mussels over wild mussels because they have a milder flavor and rarely have those pesky beards to pull out and barnacles to scrub off. This is an Italian version of a classic French dish.

1 (14 oz/398 ml) can whole peeled Italian tomatoes
1 ½ lbs (750 g) cultivated or wild mussels
2 T (30 ml) extra-light olive oil or grape seed oil
2 shallots, diced
½ small bulb fennel, trimmed and diced
4 cloves garlic, thinly sliced
1 t (5 ml) fresh thyme leaves
½ t (2 ml) chopped fresh oregano
½ t (2 ml) red pepper flakes
1 bay leaf
½ cup (125 ml) dry white wine, such as Pinot Grigio
Sea salt and freshly ground black pepper
Lemon wedges, for serving
Crusty Italian bread

Pour tomatoes into a bowl and hand-crush them, removing the hard center cores.
Alternatively, use an immersion blender to chop the tomatoes.

Scrub mussels with a brush under cold running water.
If using wild mussels, remove beards with a pair of "kitchen only" needle-nose pliers.
Refrigerate until ready to use.

In a large heavy pot or Dutch oven, heat oil over medium heat.
Add shallots and sauté for 5 minutes.
Add fennel and sauté for 5 more minutes.
Add garlic and sauté another minute.

Add the thyme, oregano, red pepper flakes, bay leaf, and crushed tomatoes.
Partially cover with a lid; reduce heat and simmer for 15 minutes.

Season the sauce to taste with salt and pepper, then add the wine and bring to a boil.
Add mussels, cover, reduce heat and simmer until shells open, about 6 to 7 minutes.
Discard any unopened mussels. Ladle into two warm bowls.

Garnish with lemon wedges and serve with crusty bread for dipping.

Serves 2

Baked Clams Oregano
Vongole Oreganata

My mother-in-law, Marie, loved this recipe. I use half plain bread crumbs and half panko bread crumbs in this recipe, which makes the breading extra crispy.

½ cup (125 ml) fresh bread crumbs
½ cup (125 ml) panko bread crumbs
½ red bell pepper, minced
2 T (30 ml) chopped fresh oregano
3 T (45 ml) chopped Italian parsley
2 T (30 ml) minced shallot
2 cloves garlic, pushed through a garlic press or minced
¼ cup (60 ml) freshly grated Parmigiano-Reggiano cheese
½ t (2 ml) paprika
½ t (2 ml) sea salt
½ t (2 ml) freshly ground black pepper
1 t (5 ml) freshly grated lemon zest
24 littleneck or cherrystone clams, shells reserved
1 T (30 ml) extra-light olive oil
½ cup (125 ml) strained clam juice, reserving any additional
Lemon wedges, for serving

In a large bowl, mix together the fresh and panko bread crumbs, red bell pepper, oregano, parsley, shallot, garlic, Parmigiano cheese, paprika, sea salt, pepper, and lemon zest.

Place clams in the freezer for 20 minutes before opening them. The cold temperature will cause the main muscle to relax, making it easier to open the shells.

Place a fine mesh sieve over a bowl and open clams over the sieve to collect the juices.
Carefully remove clams from shells and place in the sieve.
Rinse shells, and place on a rimmed baking sheet.
Roughly chop clams and spoon into the shells.

Add olive oil and strained clam juice to the bread crumb mixture and mix in.
Top each clam shell with the bread crumb mixture, packing down to secure.

Preheat oven to 425 F (220 C) degrees.

Pour about ½ cup (125 ml) of water into the bottom of the baking sheet along with any left over clam juice. This will help the clams stay moist. Bake in a 425 F (220 C) degree oven for 15 minutes.

Arrange on a warmed platter with lemon wedges and a large spoon for serving.

Serves 2 to 4

Baked Shrimp Scampi
Scampi al Forno

Shrimp come in so many sizes and are usually sold by count per pound. Here is a helpful guide.
Extra Jumbo = 16-20; Jumbo = 21-25; Extra Large = 26-30; Large = 31-35; Medium Large = 36-40;
Medium = 41-50; Small = 51-60; Extra Small = 61-70.
Serve the baked shrimp with a green salad and crusty bread and, of course, a glass of *vino bianco*.

½ cup (125 ml) panko bread crumbs
1 t (5 ml) freeze-dried or chopped fresh oregano
6 T (90 ml) unsalted butter
2 T (30 ml) extra-light olive oil
1 medium shallot, diced
4 cloves garlic, thinly sliced
1 t (5 ml) red pepper flakes
½ cup (125 ml) dry white wine
Grated zest and juice of ½ large lemon
Sea salt and freshly ground black pepper
1 lb (500 g) jumbo shrimp, peeled and deveined, tails left on

¼ cup (60 ml) freshly grated Parmigiano-Reggiano cheese
¼ cup (60 ml) chopped Italian parsley
Lemon wedges, for serving

Preheat oven to 425 F (220 C) degrees.

Mix the bread crumbs and oregano together in a small bowl.

In a small saucepan, melt the butter with the olive oil and sauté the shallot for 3 minutes.
Add the garlic and red pepper flakes and sauté another minute.
Add the wine, lemon zest, and lemon juice. Season to taste with salt and pepper.

Arrange shrimp in two individual baking dishes.
Pour the butter mixture over the shrimp, top with bread crumb mixture, and sprinkle on the grated Parmigiano cheese.

Place on a baking sheet and bake for 15 to 18 minutes, until hot and bubbly.

Sprinkle with chopped parsley and serve with lemon wedges.

Serves 2

Baked Sole with Lemon & Parmigiano

Sogliola al Forno con il Limone e Parmigiano

Sole is a delicate white fish and goes well with the bright flavors of lemon and white wine.

Bread Crumb Mixture
2 slices Italian or sourdough bread, preferably day-old
¼ cup (60 ml) freshly grated Parmigiano-Reggiano cheese
2 T (30 ml) lemon zest
½ t (2 ml) paprika
2 T (30 ml) extra-light olive oil or grape seed oil

Sole
1 ½ lbs (750 g) fillet of sole
Sea salt and freshly ground black pepper
6 T (90 ml) unsalted butter
1 clove garlic, pushed through a garlic press or minced
¼ cup (60 ml) freshly squeezed lemon juice
¼ cup (60 ml) dry white wine
2 T (30 ml) chopped Italian parsley, for garnish
Lemon wedges, for serving

Preheat oven to 400 F (200 C) degrees.

Remove crusts from bread slices and tear into pieces. Place in a food processor fitted with the steel blade; process until finely crumbled. Pour into a dry skillet and over medium heat, toast the bread crumbs to a golden brown. Let cool.
Mix the bread crumbs, Parmigiano, lemon zest, paprika, and oil together in a small bowl.

Spray oil on a large baking sheet with sides.

Rinse each fillet and pat dry with a paper towel.
Generously season with salt and pepper.
Place fillets in a single layer in the prepared baking pan.
In a small saucepan melt the butter and then add the garlic, lemon juice, and wine.
Pour most of the butter mixture over the fish, and sprinkle with the bread crumb mixture.

Bake uncovered for about 15 minutes, or until the fish flakes easily when pierced with a fork.

Using a spatula, transfer the fillets to a platter and drizzle with the rest of the butter mixture.
Sprinkle with chopped parsley and serve with lemon wedges.

Serves 4

Eggs

"Vova"

Egg-in-a-Hole

This is such a traditional Italian-American breakfast . . . a different way to serve an over-easy egg with toast. Even the hole is served!

2 thick slices Italian bread
2 eggs, preferably free-range
2 T (30 ml) unsalted butter
Salt and freshly ground black pepper
Freshly grated Parmigiano-Reggiano cheese

Cut a hole with a small cookie cutter or biscuit cutter in the center of each slice of bread.
In a skillet over medium heat, melt the butter and brown each slice of bread and hole on one side until golden.
Flip them all over and brown the other side for about a minute.
Gently crack one egg into each hole and season to taste with salt and pepper.
Cook a couple of minutes, then gently flip over and cook another minute or two, depending upon how firm you like the yolks.
Place on plates and add grated Parmigiano cheese.

Serves 1 to 2

Casa Frittata

A frittata is an egg-based dish similar to an omelette. It's an Italian version of an open-faced omelette. Frittatas are typical in the coastal region of Liguria, Italy. You can add many different types of fillings, such as bell peppers, sun-dried tomatoes, and artichokes. This one is made with potatoes, bacon, mushrooms, Fontina, and Parmigiano-Reggiano cheese. Be creative and add what you or your family likes.

2 slices bacon, diced
2 t (10 ml) extra-light olive oil
2 small potatoes, diced
1 small shallot, diced
4 cremini mushrooms, cleaned and sliced
1 T (15 ml) unsalted butter
4 eggs, preferably free-range, beaten
Salt and freshly ground black pepper
2 T (30 ml) chopped Italian parsley
2 leaves basil, chopped
2 oz (60 g) Fontina cheese, diced
Freshly grated Parmigiano-Reggiano cheese

Preheat oven to 375 F (190 C) degrees.

In an ovenproof skillet, cook the bacon over medium-high heat until crisp.
Remove bacon and set aside on a paper towel-lined plate. When cool, crumble and set aside.
In the same skillet, discard most of the bacon grease, add the olive oil and slowly cook potatoes, covered, for 10 minutes. Remove the lid and add the shallot and mushrooms and cook another 5 minutes.
Add the butter and let melt, then pour in the beaten eggs.
Season to taste with salt and pepper and sprinkle with the crumbled bacon, parsley, basil, and Fontina cheese.
Cook over low heat for a couple of minutes and then place in the oven.
Bake for about 5 to 7 minutes, until the eggs are set.
Sprinkle with grated Parmigiano cheese, cut in half or in quarters and serve.

Serves 2 to 4

Eggs in Purgatory
Uova in Purgatorio

Here is another classic Italian-American breakfast . . . eggs in tomato sauce with grated cheese and grilled Italian bread. You can use any good-quality marinara sauce from your grocery store or use my Casa Marinara Sauce (see recipe, page 64) or Casa Tomato Sauce (see recipe, page 65).

1 cup (250 ml) good-quality prepared marinara or tomato sauce
2 large eggs, preferably free-range
Salt and freshly ground black pepper
Freshly grated Parmigiano-Reggiano cheese

Preheat oven to 375 F (190 C) degrees.

Spoon a litle sauce into two small ovenproof dishes or skillets.

Break eggs into two small bowls.

Make a slight clearing in the center of the sauce by scraping with a spoon.
Carefully slide the eggs into the sauce and spoon more sauce around the eggs, but not on top.
Season to taste with salt and pepper and grated Parmigiano cheese.

Place dishes or skillets on a baking sheet. Bake for 8 to 10 minutes, until eggs are set and yolks are still soft.

Serve with crusty grilled Italian bread and additional grated Parmigiano cheese.

Serves 2

Note: You can make the recipe using two eggs for each serving—just use larger baking dishes.

Eggs Florentine
Uova Fiorentina

Eggs Florentine is another version of eggs benedict. Instead of hollandaise sauce, a cream sauce is used, and the Canadian bacon is replaced by sautéed spinach.

1 bag (10 oz/300 g) fresh baby spinach, rinsed
1 shallot, minced
2 T (30 ml) unsalted butter
1 small clove garlic, pushed through a garlic press or minced
Salt and freshly ground black pepper

172

Sauce

2 T (30 ml) unsalted butter
2 T (30 ml) flour
½ t (2 ml) dry mustard
½ t (2 ml) freshly grated nutmeg
1 cup (250 ml) milk
2 T (30 ml) freshly grated Parmigiano-Reggiano cheese, plus more for finishing
Salt and freshly ground black pepper

4 eggs, preferably free-range
1 t (5 ml) salt
1 T (15 ml) white vinegar
2 pinches cayenne pepper

Put a little water in a large skillet and slowly steam the spinach for 2 to 3 minutes. Stir after a minute. Pour into a strainer and when cool enough to handle, squeeze out the water, chop and place in a bowl.
Wipe out the skillet with a paper towel and over low heat, sauté the shallot in the 2 tablespoons (30 ml) butter for 5 minutes.
Add the garlic, season to taste with salt and pepper, and cook another minute.
Add the spinach and stir to combine. Divide the spinach mixture between two small ovenproof dishes or skillets.

In a small saucepan over medium-low heat, melt the butter until it begins to foam, add the flour, dry mustard, and nutmeg and whisk for 1 minute. Slowly whisk in the milk and cook for about 3 minutes, or until thickened. Whisk in the grated cheese, season to taste with salt and pepper, and keep warm.

Break the eggs into 4 individual saucers.
Fill a large skillet half full with water and bring to a simmer.
Add the salt and vinegar and slip eggs into the simmering water. Cover and remove from the heat.
Allow to sit for 2 minutes. Gently turn each egg over in the water. Cover and let sit another 1 to 2 minutes.

Preheat broiler and remove eggs from skillet with a slotted spoon; gently place two on top of the spinach in each baking dish. Spoon on some of the sauce and add a little grated cheese and a pinch of cayenne pepper.
Set dishes on a baking sheet and place under the broiler for about 1 or 2 minutes, until the sauce is hot.
Serve with crusty grilled Italian bread.

Serves 2

Side Dishes

"Contorni"

Eggplant Parmigiana
Melanzane alla Parmigiana

The eggplant in my version of eggplant parmigiana resembles southern-style fried green tomatoes, with all the crunch—and they are not fried. For this recipe, you stack them together and bake a final time for about 10 minutes, until the cheese melts. I ordered this as a lunch, one stack only, at Ristorante Tre Sorelle (Three Sisters) in Positano, Italy. I have been making eggplant parmigiana like this ever since.

4 cups (1 litre) chicken stock
2 t (10 ml) saffron threads (optional)
2 T (30 ml) extra-light olive oil or grape seed oil
1 thin slice pancetta (optional)
2 medium shallots, minced
1 clove garlic, minced
1 ½ cups (375 ml) Arborio rice
½ cup (125 ml) dry white wine, such as Pinot Grigio
Salt and freshly ground black pepper
4 T (60 ml) unsalted butter, cut into cubes
½ cup (125 ml) freshly grated Parmigiano-Reggiano cheese
1 T (1 ml) fresh lemon juice

Pour the chicken stock in a saucepan along with the saffron threads (if using) and bring to a boil. Reduce heat and keep hot at a very low temperature on the stove.

In a large skillet over medium heat, add the oil.
Add the pancetta and sauté for 5 minutes; remove and discard it.
Add shallots and sauté for 5 minutes, until translucent.
Add garlic and sauté another minute.
Add rice and sauté another 2 minutes, while stirring.
Add wine and cook while stirring until wine is absorbed, about 3 minutes.

Reduce heat to low and add hot chicken stock (one ladle at a time), stirring with a wooden spoon until the liquid is absorbed. Keep doing this until the rice is tender but firm (al dente) and creamy, and the stock is all used up; this takes about 25 minutes over low heat.

Risotto should be a little bit soupy. If you find it too dry, you can add ½ cup (125 ml) of water near the end of the cooking process.

Season to taste with salt and pepper.
Stir in the butter, Parmigiano cheese, and lemon juice.

Serve immediately.

Serves 4

Peas with Pancetta

Piselli con Pancetta

Are you tired of boring peas? Here is a way to add lots of flavor—plus, it's easy to make.

4 oz (125 g) pancetta, diced
1 T (15 ml) extra-light olive oil
3 shallots, halved and thinly sliced
2 cloves garlic, minced
Pinch of red pepper flakes
1 lb (500 g) frozen peas, thawed
Salt and freshly ground black pepper

In a skillet or saucepan over medium heat, add the pancetta and cook until crisp.
With a slotted spoon, transfer the pancetta to a plate and set aside.
Add olive oil to the skillet or pan and sauté the shallots for 5 minutes.
Add the garlic and red pepper flakes and sauté another minute.
Add the peas and cook 5 more minutes, while stirring.
Season to taste with salt and pepper and return the pancetta to the pan; lightly stir to combine.

Serves 4

Scalloped Potatoes with Quattro Formaggi
Patate ai Quattro Formaggi

Use any variety of Italian cheeses that you prefer. This side dish goes well with so many meat, poultry or seafood dishes.

2 oz (60 g) Asiago cheese,
  finely chopped
2 oz (60 g) Fontina cheese,
  finely chopped
2 oz (60 g) Parmigiano-Reggiano
  cheese, grated
2 oz (60 g) Pecorino Romano
  cheese, grated
2 T (30 ml) extra-light olive oil
1 medium onion, cut in half
  and thinly sliced
1 clove garlic, minced
1 lb (500 g) Yukon Gold potatoes, peeled and thinly sliced with a mandoline or knife
Salt and freshly ground black pepper
½ t (2 ml) freshly ground nutmeg
¼ cup (60 ml) whole milk or half-and-half (half cream)
2 T (30 ml) unsalted butter

Preheat oven to 375 F (190 C) degrees.

Place grated cheeses in a bowl and mix well by hand.

In a skillet, add the oil and sauté the onion for 5 minutes.
Add the garlic and sauté another minute. Turn off heat and set aside.

Brush a gratin dish with a little more olive oil and arrange half of the potatoes in the dish,
slightly overlapping slices. Sprinkle with some salt, pepper, and nutmeg. Add the onion mixture and
half of the cheese mixture.
Repeat with the remaining potatoes, salt, pepper, nutmeg, and cheese.
Place the dish on a baking sheet, pour the milk or half-and-half over the potatoes, and dot with
butter.

Bake until golden brown and potatoes are fork tender, about 30 to 35 minutes.

Serves 4

Baked Zucchini
Zucchine al Forno

My son Brandon and daughter Angie always loved the deep-fried zucchini at our favorite Italian restaurant in Bethesda, Maryland. I eventually started baking eggplant for eggplant parmigiana and it always turned out crisp and light. I developed this recipe using zucchini slices and found that it makes a great side dish or antipasto.

½ cup (125 ml) panko bread crumbs
¼ cup (60 ml) dry plain bread crumbs
¼ cup (60 ml) freshly grated Parmigiano-Reggiano cheese
½ t (2 ml) garlic powder
Salt and freshly ground black pepper
½ cup (125 ml) extra-light olive oil or grape seed oil
2 small to medium zucchini, washed and sliced diagonally into ¼-inch (6-mm) slices.

Preheat oven to 425 F (220 C) degrees.

In a shallow bowl, combine the panko bread crumbs, dry bread crumbs, Parmigiano cheese, and garlic powder. Season to taste with salt and pepper.

Pour the oil into another shallow bowl and dip the zucchini slices, one at a time, into the oil and then press the oiled zucchini into the bread crumb mixture.

Place slices on a baking sheet fitted with a rack.

Bake for 25 minutes or until golden.

Transfer to a platter and serve with lemon wedges.

Serves 4

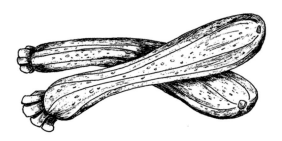

Asparagus with Prosciutto & Parmigiano

Asparagi con Prosciutto e Parmigiano

If you are tired of asparagus spears with hollandaise sauce, then this is a delicious and quick alternative.

1 lb (500 g) asparagus, ends trimmed
2 t (10 ml) sea salt
2 T (30 ml) unsalted butter, melted
Freshly ground black pepper
¼ lb (125 g) Prosciutto di Parma, cut into thin strips
Parmigiano-Reggiano cheese, shaved

In a large skillet, add water to half full. Bring to a boil and then add the salt. Stir and add the asparagus, lined up in one direction.
Gently boil, uncovered, until the asparagus are just tender, about 5 minutes.
Using tongs, carefully transfer the asparagus to a serving dish and drizzle with melted butter.
Garnish with the Prosciutto, a few pieces of shaved Parmigiano cheese, and some black pepper.

Serves 4

Green Beans
Fagioli Verdi

This is my daughter Angie's favorite way to have green beans. I have been making this recipe for 20 years. It cooks quickly, so have everything prepped and set aside on a cutting board.

1 t (5 ml) sea salt
1 ½ lbs (750 g) green beans, trimmed
2 small shallots, thinly sliced
1 large clove garlic, thinly sliced
¼ cup (60 ml) extra-light olive oil or grape seed oil
8 cherry tomatoes, diced
¼ cup (60 ml) dry white wine
¼ cup (60 ml) pitted and chopped Italian black olives
Salt and freshly ground black pepper
2 t (10 ml) finely grated lemon zest

In a large skillet, add water to half full. Bring to a boil, add the salt and green beans; cover and simmer for about 3 minutes. Drain and set aside.
In the same skillet, sauté the shallots and garlic in the oil over low heat for 3 to 4 minutes.
Add the tomatoes, green beans, wine, and olives. Season to taste with salt and pepper.
Simmer for a couple for minutes while gently stirring.
Transfer to a serving bowl and sprinkle with lemon zest.

Serves 4

Mamaw's Stuffed Peppers
Peperoni Ripieni

Campania, in the southern part of Italy, is known for growing incredible tomatoes and sweet bell peppers. The soil is very fertile because of the still-active volcano, Mount Vesuvius (Monte Vesuvio, in Italian). Elisabeth Greco Noviello, aka Mamaw, made these stuffed peppers often. She served them as a main course and used only green bell peppers. It was very economical for her family of six during the Great Depression in the early 1930s. I've spruced it up a bit using red, green, orange, and yellow bell peppers, but use one color if you prefer.

This recipe serves 4 as a side dish, or 2 as a main dish.

Be sure to use only fresh breadcrumbs—it makes all the difference.

6 slices Italian or sourdough bread, preferably day-old
4 medium bell peppers, assorted colors
¼ cup (60 ml) extra-light olive oil or grape seed oil, divided
¼ cup (60 ml) diced onion
2 cloves garlic, minced
2 T (30 ml) unsalted butter
½ cup (125 ml) freshly grated Parmigiano-Reggiano cheese
¼ cup (60 ml) freshly grated Pecorino Romano cheese
¼ cup (60 ml) chopped Italian parsley
2 T (30 ml) chopped fresh basil
1 t (5 ml) freeze-dried or chopped fresh oregano
Salt and freshly ground black pepper

Preheat oven to 375 F (190 C) degrees.

Tear up the slices of bread and place in a food processor. Pulse to make medium-fine bread crumbs. You should have about 2 cups (500 ml) of bread crumbs.

Cut off tops of bell peppers and clean out the inside of the shells.
Slightly trim the bottoms so that the peppers stand up.
Mince about 1 tablespoon (15 ml) of each of the bell pepper tops and set aside.
Spray a baking pan with cooking oil and stand the peppers in the pan.

Heat 2 tablespoons (30 ml) of the oil in a skillet; add the onion and minced bell peppers and sauté for 10 minutes.
Add the garlic and sauté another minute.
Lower the heat and stir in the butter and bread crumbs.
Remove from heat and add the rest of the ingredients.

Fill the pepper halves with the stuffing mixture, packing tightly, then drizzle with the remaining 2 tablespoons oil.
Bake for about 55 to 60 minutes, until the tops are golden brown and the peppers are soft but not falling apart.

Serve hot or at room temperature.

Serves 2 to 4

Ted's Sautéed Mushrooms
Funghi Saltati

I never liked mushrooms until I had my father-in-law's sautéed mushrooms. He used garlic powder instead of minced garlic. I didn't change a thing because they turn out perfect every time, each mushroom delicately flavored with the garlic powder. The little bit of red pepper flakes adds just enough heat, and the parsley is for a little color.

1 lb (500 g) white or cremini mushrooms
3 T (45 ml) extra-light olive oil or grape seed oil
1 t (5 ml) garlic powder
1 t (5 ml) red pepper flakes
Salt and freshly ground black pepper
Italian parsley, minced

Wipe mushrooms clean with a damp cloth.
Cut off the very ends of the stems and slice each mushroom into 4 to 5 slices.

Heat oil over medium-high heat in a large skillet.
Add the mushrooms and stir with a wooden spoon while cooking.
The mushrooms will release water, but keep cooking and stirring over medium-high heat.
The water will eventually evaporate and you can add a little more olive oil.
Keep this up until the mushrooms start to brown slightly.
Add the garlic powder, red pepper flakes, and season to taste with salt and pepper.

This whole procedure takes about 20 minutes.

Spoon into a bowl and sprinkle with some parsley flakes.

Serve this as a side dish with steak or roasted chicken.

Serves 4

Ted Casazza
with grandson Brandon

Sweets

"Dolci"

Raspberry Jam-Filled Heart Cookies
Marmellata di Lamponi Biscotti del Cuore

I usually make these cookies during Christmas using star-shaped cookie cutters, and sometimes I add poppy seeds to the dough. These heart-shaped cookies make great little treats for Valentine's Day.

1 cup (250 ml) unsalted butter (2 sticks), room temperature
½ cup (125 ml) granulated sugar
2 large egg yolks
1 t (5 ml) pure vanilla extract
2 cups (500 ml) all-purpose flour
Raspberry jam
Confectioners' sugar, for dusting

Preheat oven to 350 F (180 C) degrees. Lightly grease 2 cookie sheets.

In the bowl of an electric mixer fitted with the paddle, mix butter and sugar until light and fluffy. Add the egg yolks and vanilla and beat to completely incorporate. Mix in the flour, a little at a time, until well combined.

Turn dough out onto a lightly floured surface and divide into two equal pieces.
Form each piece into a disc, wrap in plastic, and refrigerate for at least one hour.

On a lightly floured surface, working with one piece at a time, roll dough ¼-inch (6-mm) thick.

Use a 2 ½-inch (6.35-cm) cookie cutter (heart-shaped or other shape of your choice) to cut out cookies.
Transfer to baking sheets. Use a smaller cookie cutter to cut out the centers of half of the cookies. The cut-out cookies are the tops.

Bake for 10 to 12 minutes.

Bake the small center cut-outs and also dust with confectioners' sugar for a baker's treat.

Transfer to wire racks and cool completely.

When ready to assemble, place the cut-out cookies back on the baking sheets and generously dust with confectioners' sugar.

Spread about ½ teaspoon (2 ml) of jam on all the solid cookies and gently top with the sugared cut-out cookie.

Makes about 3 dozen (36) cookies

Chocolate Hazelnut Biscotti
Cioccolato Nocciola Biscotti

This is an adult dessert, but if you want to serve these biscotti to children, leave out the espresso powder and liqueur.

1 cup (250 ml) hazelnuts
4 oz (125 g) fine-quality bittersweet or semisweet chocolate (preferably 70% cacao), chopped
1 cup (250 ml) firmly packed dark brown sugar
¼ cup (60 ml) granulated sugar
2 cups (500 ml) all-purpose flour
¾ cup (175 ml) unsweetened cocoa powder
1 T (15 ml) instant espresso powder
1 t (5 ml) baking soda
½ t (2 ml) salt
3 large eggs
2 t (10 ml) pure vanilla extract
1 T (15 ml) hazelnut liqueur such as Frangelico (optional)

Preheat oven to 350 F (180 C) degrees.

Spread hazelnuts on a baking sheet and bake for about 15 minutes or until lightly browned. Remove from oven and wrap them in a clean dish towel. Let them steam for about 5 minutes. Briskly rub the towel with both hands to remove most of the skins from the nuts.

When cool, place nuts on a cutting board, coarsely chop, then set aside in a small bowl.

In a food processor fitted with the metal blade, add the chopped chocolate, brown sugar, and granulated sugar; process until the chocolate is very fine.

In a large bowl, whisk together the flour, cocoa powder, espresso powder, baking soda, and salt. Add the chocolate-sugar mixture and whisk together to combine.

In the bowl of an electric mixer fitted with the paddle, add the eggs and vanilla and mix to combine.

Slowly add the dry mixture to the mixer and mix another minute or two. Remove bowl from mixer and use a wooden spoon to stir in the hazelnuts and liqueur.

Shape dough with lightly floured hands into a log measuring 12 by 3 inches (30 by 7.5 cm). Place on a lightly oiled baking sheet and bake for 40 minutes.

Remove from oven and let cool until you can handle it. Use a serrated knife and cut into ½-inch (12-mm) slices. Place cookies on their sides on the baking sheet.

Lower the temperature to 325 F (170 C) and bake for 15 minutes.

Carefully flip the cookies over and bake another 15 minutes.

Let cool on a wire rack and store in an airtight container.

Makes about 2 dozen (24) cookies.

Lady Kisses
Baci di Dama

These cookies are great at Christmas or any time of the year. They are also delicious by substituting ground almonds for about one-quarter of the flour.

Cookies
1 cup (250 ml) unsalted butter (2 sticks), room temperature
¾ cup (175 ml) confectioners' sugar
½ t (2 ml) salt
2 T (30 ml) Frangelico, Kahlua, or dark rum (optional)
2 cups (500 ml) all-purpose flour

Preheat oven to 350 F (180 C) degrees.

In the bowl of an electric mixer fitted with the paddle, beat together the butter, confectioners' sugar, and salt until light and fluffy. Blend in the liqueur and beat in the flour, until well blended. Cover and refrigerate for at least one hour.

Pinch off pieces of dough, about ½ teaspoon (2 ml) each, and roll into balls.
Place about 1-inch (2.5-cm) apart on ungreased baking sheets.

Bake for 14 to 15 minutes, or until lightly golden. Transfer to a wire rack and cool completely.

Chocolate Filling
4 oz (125 g) fine-quality bittersweet or semisweet chocolate (preferably 70% cacao), chopped
2 T (30 ml) unsalted butter
Pinch of salt

While cookies are cooling, place chopped chocolate into a bowl that will fit snugly on top of a saucepan.
Heat some water in the saucepan until it simmers. Turn off heat and place the bowl of chocolate over the water. Let the chocolate melt, and then stir it gently with a plastic spatula.
Remove from heat and stir in the butter. Let cool.

Turn half of the cookies over and, using a kitchen knife, spread a small amount of the chocolate on the bottom of half of the cookies.

Place the bottom of a second cookie against the chocolate, sandwich style, and press very lightly together.

Store in an airtight container for a week or more.

These are excellent served with espresso or milk.

Makes about 3 dozen (36) cookies.

Christmas Pignoli Cookies
Natali Pignoli Biscotti

Pine nuts (pignoli) can be found in all grocery stores now. It takes a little extra time to place the nuts securely on the dough but it's quite therapeutic. I sat down at my kitchen counter and watched an old Christmas movie while making these. This is the Italian version of Jewish macaroons that are served at Passover. Keep a bowl of water nearby to dip your hands in to get rid of the stickiness and then dry them. This will keep the nuts from completely sticking to your fingers.

2 (8 oz/250 g) cans almond paste
¾ cup (175 ml) granulated sugar
¼ cup (60 ml) confectioners' sugar
½ cup (125 ml) almond flour
½ t (2 ml) almond extract
2 egg whites
Finely grated zest of 1 orange
1 ½ cups (375 ml) pine nuts

Using a spoon, scoop the almond paste into the bowl of a food processor fitted with the steel blade and process until crumbly.
Add the sugars and process until combined.
Add the almond flour, almond extract, egg whites, and orange zest through the feed tube while the motor is running.

Pour about half of the pine nuts into a shallow bowl and set aside. You may need all of the nuts but start with a portion.

Make (1-inch/2.5-cm) balls of dough and dip the top of each ball into the pine nuts.
Place on a lightly oiled baking sheet and press on the nuts to secure, placing on a few more nuts, if needed.

Preheat oven to 350 F (180 C) degrees.

Bake in center of oven for 20 minutes, or until golden brown. Let cool 5 minutes, then transfer to a wire rack to cool completely.

Store in cookie tins and hide them until Christmas! The cookies will keep well for about 2 weeks.

Makes about 3 dozen (36) cookies.

Espresso Panna Cotta

The French have crème caramel and the Spanish have flan. In the Piedmont region of Italy, panna cotta is also known as *dolce a cucchiaio,* or "spoon dessert." You can cut down on the calories a little bit by exchanging whole milk for the half-and-half, but you really need the richness of some cream in panna cotta—remember it doesn't have eggs like a custard and besides, the portions are only about a half cup. I like to pour the mixture into small martini glasses . . . no unmolding necessary.

2 ½ t (12 ml) powdered unflavored
   gelatin (1 packet)
2 cups (500 ml) half-and-half
   (half cream)
¼ cup (60 ml) granulated sugar
1 T (15 ml) instant espresso powder

2 T (30 ml) toasted and crushed
   hazelnuts
1 dark chocolate bar, slightly warm*

Pour the half-and-half into a small saucepan. Sprinkle in the powdered gelatin and let stand for a couple of minutes to soften.
Set the saucepan over medium heat just until the gelatin dissolves, but do not let the mixture boil. Stir in the sugar and espresso powder and continue to stir over medium heat until the sugar dissolves, about 3 more minutes. Turn off heat and let cool slightly.
Pour into 4 martini glasses or small ramekins. Cover and refrigerate 6 to 8 hours.

When ready to serve, use a vegetable peeler to shave some chocolate from the chocolate bar into a small bowl.
Sprinkle on some hazelnuts in the center of each dessert and add a little of the shaved chocolate.

* If the chocolate bar is slightly warmer than room temperature, it will be easier to shave.

Serves 4

Broiled Zabaglione Over Fruit
Zabaglione al Forno su Frutta

Zabaglione is an Italian unset custard, pronounced "zah bahl YOH nay." In French cooking it is called sabayon. Using a hand-held electric mixer, it takes a few minutes to thicken. Spoon some fruit into crème brûlée dishes, drizzle on some zabaglione and put under the broiler for a few seconds. Traditionally zabaglione it is made with Marsala wine, but I prefer it with Limoncello, which is mainly produced in Southern Italy from Naples to Salerno. Use any fruit of your choice. Here I used blueberries, blackberries, strawberries, and raspberries.

3 cups (750 ml) mixed
   fresh berries
3 T (45 ml) granulated
   sugar
4 large egg yolks
¼ cup (60 ml) granulated
   sugar
Pinch of sea salt
2 t (10 ml) grated lemon
   zest
¼ cup (60 ml) limoncello (a sweet Italian lemon liqueur)

In a bowl, toss the berries with the 3 tablespoons of sugar and spoon into 4 ramekins or crème brûlée dishes. Place on a baking sheet and set aside.

Combine the egg yolks, sugar, sea salt, lemon zest, and limoncello in a large metal or glass bowl. Using an electric hand mixer, mix vigorously until slightly thickened and the color is pale yellow. Set the bowl over a saucepan of simmering water, being careful not to let the bowl touch the water. On high speed, mix again until it has tripled in volume and is thick and creamy, about 5 minutes.

Spoon some of the zabaglione over the fruit.
Place under broiler for 30 to 45 seconds. Don't walk away as it burns very quickly.

Serves 4

Sicilian Espresso Gelato

Sicilian gelato typically does not use eggs or cream and therefore contains less butterfat than ice cream. It is stabilized by adding cornstarch in place of the eggs. For a creamy texture, use whole milk.

4 cups (1 litre) whole milk
2 T (30 ml) cornstarch
¾ cup (175 ml) granulated sugar
1 T (15 ml) coffee liqueur (Kahlua or Tia Maria)
¼ cup (60 ml) instant espresso powder, or more to taste

In a small bowl, make a slurry by mixing ¼ cup (60 ml) of the milk with the cornstarch. Whisk until smooth.
In a medium saucepan, bring the milk to a simmer, then remove from the heat.
Add the sugar and the cornstarch mixture and stir. Return to a simmer for about 2 minutes.
Remove from heat and add the coffee liqueur and espresso powder. Stir to combine.

Let cool and then pour into a covered container and refrigerate until completely chilled.
Pour the mixture into an ice cream maker and freeze, according to the manufacturer's instructions.
Transfer to a covered container and place in your freezer, until firm.

Serves 4

Sicilian Pistachio Gelato

Pistachio nuts are known to reduce levels of LDL and increase the antioxidant levels in our blood plasma. Moderation is the key . . . indulge once in a while.

4 cups (1 litre) whole milk
2 T (30 ml) cornstarch
¾ cup (175 ml) granulated sugar
1 t (5 ml) almond extract
2 cups (500 ml) shelled unsalted
    pistachio nuts

Preheat oven to 350 F (180 C) degrees.
Place pistachios on a baking sheet and bake for 4 to 5 minutes.

When cool, chop about ½ cup (125 ml) of nuts and set them aside.
Process the rest in a food processor fitted with the steel blade, until crumbled, but not made into butter.

In a small bowl, make a slurry by mixing ¼ cup (60 ml) of the milk with the cornstarch. Whisk until smooth.

In a medium saucepan, bring the milk to a simmer, then remove from the heat.
Add the sugar and the cornstarch mixture and stir. Return to a simmer for about 2 minutes.
Remove from heat and add the almond extract and ground nuts. Stir to combine.

Let cool and then pour into a covered container and refrigerate until completely chilled.
Pour the mixture into an ice cream maker and freeze, according to the manufacturer's instructions.
Transfer to a covered container and place in your freezer, until firm.

Garnish with some of the chopped pistachios.

Serves 4

Strawberry-Raspberry Sorbet
Sorbetto di Fragole e Lamponi

Make this sorbet when strawberries and raspberries are in season and at their best flavor. In early summer, I can buy strawberries from a farm nearby and organic raspberries at the farmers' market in town. This is such a refreshing dessert and is so full of sweet, ripe fruit flavor.

1 lb (500 g) fresh strawberries
8 oz (250 g) fresh raspberries
1 t (5 ml) fresh lemon juice
2 T (30 ml) Fragoli (wild strawberry liqueur), optional
¾ cup (175 ml) granulated sugar
¾ cup (175 ml) water

Trim the stems from the strawberries and cut in half.
Pour the strawberries and raspberries into a food processor or blender and puree.
Pour into a fine mesh strainer set over a bowl and press the juice through with a wooden spoon.
Discard the berry pulp and seeds that remain in the strainer.
Stir in the lemon juice and Fragoli, if using.
In a medium saucepan, heat the sugar and water until the sugar dissolves. Set aside to cool.
Pour the sugar syrup into the bowl with the berry puree and stir to combine.
Cover with plastic wrap and refrigerate until completely chilled.
Pour the mixture into an ice cream maker and freeze, according to the manufacturer's instructions.
Transfer to a covered container and place in your freezer, until firm.

Serves 4

Strawberries with Balsamic Vinegar
Fragole con Aceto Balsamico

Strawberries and balsamic vinegar are amazing together . . . even better with vanilla ice cream or gelato.

1 lb (500g) fresh strawberries, hulled and sliced
2 T (30 ml) granulated sugar, divided
1 T (15 ml) finely grated orange zest
¼ cup (60 ml) good-quality balsamic vinegar
2 T (30 ml) fresh orange juice
Fresh mint leaves, for garnish

Place the strawberries in a bowl and sprinkle with 1 tablespoon of the sugar and the grated orange zest. Set aside.
Heat the balsamic vinegar, remaining 1 tablespoon sugar, and orange juice in a small saucepan, stirring until combined. Remove from heat and let cool.

Pour the cooled balsamic vinegar mixture over the strawberries. Cover and refrigerate until well chilled.
Serve with vanilla ice cream or gelato and fresh mint leaves, for garnish.

Serves 4

Peaches with Mascarpone Cheese & Amaretto
Pesche con Mascarpone e Amaretti

Amaretti cookies are Italian macaroon cookies that originated in Venice, Italy, during the Renaissance era. You can buy them at Italian specialty grocers or even order them online. Amaretto is a sweet, almond-flavored Italian liqueur. Here is a dessert using very ripe peaches, mascarpone cheese, whipped cream, amaretto liqueur, amaretti cookies, and sliced almonds . . . a perfect combination.

3 large ripe peaches, peeled, pitted and cut into chunks
¼ cup (60 ml) amaretto liqueur
1 T (15 ml) freshly squeezed lemon juice
8 small amaretti cookies
6 oz (185 g) mascarpone, room temperature
¼ cup (60 ml) granulated sugar
1 cup (250 ml) heavy cream
¼ cup (60 ml) sliced almonds

Put peaches into a bowl and add the amaretto and lemon juice.
Gently toss to coat and set aside.

Place cookies in a zippered plastic bag and seal.
Gently crush with a mallet or rolling pin. Pour into a small bowl and set aside.

In a large bowl, whisk together the mascarpone and sugar until well blended and fluffy.
In another bowl, with a hand-held mixer, whip the cream until stiff peaks form.

Using a rubber spatula, fold the whipped cream into the mascarpone mixture just until combined.
Place a spoonful of the peaches along with some juice into each of 4 parfait or ice cream dishes.
Spoon some of the mascarpone-cream mixture on top of the peaches.
Repeat with more peaches and juice, ending with the mascarpone-cream on top.
Chill until ready to serve.

Before serving, sprinkle on the crushed amaretti cookies and top with sliced almonds.

Serves 4

Lemon Sorbet with Prosecco
Sgroppino al Limone

Traditionally, *sgroppino* is a refreshing aperitif that is said to have originated in Venice, Italy, and is served blended, but this is another way to serve it as a dessert. With the abundance of lemons on the Amalfi Coast, I think it could have been invented there. This is so refreshing on a warm summer evening.

1 cup (250 ml) chilled Prosecco
¼ cup (60 ml) chilled limoncello (a sweet Italian lemon liqueur)
¼ cup (60 ml) chilled plain or lemon-flavored vodka
Good-quality lemon sorbet
Fresh mint leaves

Pour ½ cup (125 ml) Prosecco into each champagne flute or Irish coffee glass.
Equally divide the limoncello and vodka into each flute or glass.
Add 2 to 3 scoops of lemon sorbet.
Top with mint and and serve immediately.

Serves 2

Affogato

Affogato is a coffee-based ice cream dessert that is so refreshing, especially on a warm summer evening. Affogato translates to "drowned in coffee" in Italian. It's such an easy dessert to put together, especially if you have instant espresso powder in your pantry.

1 cup (250 ml) brewed espresso
(or use instant espresso powder)
8 small amaretti cookies
½ cup (125 ml) heavy whipping cream
Vanilla gelato or ice cream
Amaretto liqueur
¼ cup (40 g) sliced almonds

Brew the espresso and set aside to cool, or use instant espresso powder to make 1 cup strong coffee.
Place cookies in a zippered plastic bag and seal.
Gently crush with a mallet or rolling pin. Pour into a small bowl and set aside.

Make the Vanilla Whipped Cream (see below) and refrigerate.

Set out 4 ice cream dishes or martini glasses.
Add 2 scoops of vanilla gelato or ice cream to each glass.
Pour about ¼ cup (60 ml) cooled espresso over each, drizzle with Amaretto liqueur, and add the crumbled cookies. Finish with a dollop of whipped cream and top with almonds. Serve immediately.

Vanilla Whipped Cream
½ cup (125 ml) heavy whipping cream, chilled
A splash of pure vanilla extract
1 t (5 ml) granulated sugar

Whip cream until soft peaks form. Add the vanilla and sugar and whip until stiffer peaks form.

Serves 4

Peach, Cherry & Blueberry Crostata
Crostata di Pesche, Ciliegie e Mirtilli

You don't need a pie pan for this recipe because it's a rustic Italian pie. This is definitely "easy as pie." Use any combination of fruit you prefer.

Pastry
2 cups (500 ml) all-purpose flour
2 T (30 ml) granulated sugar
½ t (2 ml) salt
Grated zest of ½ lemon
½ cup (125 ml) cold unsalted butter (1 stick), cut into pieces
4 to 5 T ice-cold water

Put the flour, sugar, and salt in a food processor fitted with the steel blade. Pulse until combined.
Add lemon zest and butter and pulse until butter pieces are the size of peas.
Through the feed tube, slowly add water and process briefly until mixture comes together.
Transfer dough onto a large piece of plastic wrap and wrap up, flattening and forming the dough into a disc.

Refrigerate at least one hour before rolling out.
While pastry is chilling, make the filling.

Filling
2 ripe peaches, pitted and thinly sliced
½ cup (125 ml) fresh cherries, pitted and cut in half
½ cup (125 ml) fresh blueberries
Juice of ½ lemon
½ cup (125 ml) granulated sugar
1 T (15 ml) flour
2 T (30 ml) unsalted butter, cut into pieces

Combine the peaches, cherries, blueberries, lemon juice, sugar, and flour in a bowl and mix gently to combine.

Preheat oven to 375 F (190 C) degrees.

Remove dough from refrigerator and allow to soften for 10 minutes.
Roll the dough out onto a lightly floured surface into a 14-inch (35-cm) circle. Roll it onto and around your rolling pin and place on a parchment-lined baking sheet with sides.

Spoon filling into center and fold edges of dough over filling, leaving center uncovered. Dot the exposed fruit with butter.

Brush crust with cream or milk and dust with sugar.
Bake for about one hour, or until fruit is bubbling and crust is golden brown.

Let cool before serving. Serve with whipped cream, vanilla gelato, or vanilla ice cream.

Serves 4 to 6

Pear Tart

Crostata di Pere

Mascarpone is a creamy Italian cheese made from cow's milk. The cows are fed special grasses supplemented with herbs and flowers so they produce milk that is perfect for making this cheese. Mascarpone cheese can be found in grocery stores in 8-ounce (250-g) containers.

1 ¼ cups (310 ml) pastry or all-purpose flour
¼ cup (60 ml) granulated sugar
1 t (5 ml) finely grated lemon zest
Pinch of salt
4 T (60 ml) cold unsalted butter (½ stick), cut into pieces
1 egg yolk
¼ cup (60 ml) cold cream or half-and-half (half cream)

Place the flour, sugar, lemon zest, and salt in the bowl of a food processor fitted with the steel blade. Pulse for a few seconds to combine.
Add the butter and pulse a few more seconds.
In a bowl, whisk the egg yolk and cream until combined.
With the motor running, pour the egg yolk mixture down the feed tube and pulse just until the dough comes together.

Turn out onto a large piece of plastic wrap. Wrap up, flattening and forming the dough into a disc. Chill for at least one hour.

Preheat oven to 375 F (190 C) degrees.

Lightly dust your work surface with flour and roll the pastry out to fit a 9-inch (23-cm), removable-bottom tart pan. Press the dough carefully up the sides, then roll off overhang with your rolling pin and remove.
Cut a round piece of parchment paper, to fit in the bottom and up the sides of the dough. Place over the dough and add about 2 cups (500 ml) pie weights or dried beans on top of the parchment paper. Bake the crust for 20 minutes.
Let cool slightly and remove paper and weights.

Mascarpone Cheese Filling
¾ cup (175 ml) mascarpone, room temperature
¼ cup (60 ml) granulated sugar
1 egg
½ t (2 ml) pure vanilla extract
1 T (15 ml) flour

In a medium bowl, stir together the mascarpone cheese, sugar, egg, vanilla, and flour until well combined. Pour into the cooled tart shell and smooth the surface.

3 medium-size ripe Anjou or Bosc pears
¼ cup (60 ml) unsalted hazelnuts, chopped
2 T (30 ml) granulated sugar

3 T (45 ml) apricot jelly
2 T (30 ml) Calvados or peach brandy

Preheat oven to 325 F (160 C) degrees.

Peel and cut the pears in half and remove core with a melon baller or a spoon.
Arrange in the tart shell with narrower ends pointing towards center.
If necessary, trim the pears to fit into the tart.
Scatter the hazelnuts over the pears and sprinkle the sugar on top.
Place on a baking sheet and bake for 55 to 60 minutes, until golden and the pears are soft.

Heat the apricot jelly in a small saucepan, or microwave it just until warm.
Turn off heat and add the Calvados or peach brandy and mix to combine.
Brush over the pears.

Serve warm or at room temperature.

Serves 6

Chocolate Pistachio Tart
Crostata al Cioccolato-Pistacchio

This is a quick refrigerator tart. The only part that is baked is the crust. You can add any liqueur you prefer or none at all. If you want to use chopped hazelnuts instead of pistachios, try using Frangelico liqueur to complement their flavor.

Crust
¼ cup (60 ml) unsalted butter, cut into pieces
10 small amaretti cookies
¼ cup (60 ml) firmly packed dark brown sugar

Filling
12 oz (375 g) fine-quality bittersweet or semisweet chocolate (preferably 70% cacao), chopped
1 cup (250 ml) heavy cream
1 cup (250 ml) chopped pistachio nuts, divided
2 T (30 ml) pistachio liqueur or Grand Marnier (optional)

Lightly butter the bottom and sides of a 9-inch (23-cm) springform pan.

Preheat oven to 350 F (180 C) degrees.

In a food processor fitted with the steel blade, combine the butter, cookies, and sugar.
Process until the mixture forms moist crumbs and sticks together.
Press the crumb mixture into the bottom of the prepared springform pan.

Bake for 10 minutes, or until golden.

Cool to room temperature.

Transfer the chopped chocolate into a heatproof bowl.
Heat the cream in a small saucepan over medium heat to just below the boiling point.
Pour the hot cream into the bowl. Let stand for 1 minute, then stir mixture until chocolate is melted and mixture is smooth.

Add ½ cup (125 ml) of the pistachios and the liqueur.
Pour the chocolate filling into the springform pan; cover and refrigerate for at least 8 hours.

Unmold tart by running a table knife around edges.
Remove rim and place the tart on a serving plate.
Sprinkle with the remaining ½ cup (125 ml) of the pistachios.

Serves 6 to 8

Apple Torta
Torta di Mele

Many countries have their own version of an apple cake. Mamaw used to make this for family gatherings. The only extra ingredients I've added are the apple brandy and lemon zest, but you don't have to use them. Either way, this cake is amazingly moist and delicious . . . even great for breakfast.

Softened butter
3 large Golden Delicious or Honeycrisp apples
½ cup (125 ml) unsalted butter (1 stick)
¾ cup (175 ml) pastry or all-purpose flour
½ t (2 ml) baking powder
½ t (2 ml) salt
3 large eggs
1 t (5 ml) pure vanilla extract
1 T (15 ml) apple-flavored brandy, such as Calvados (optional)
1 cup (250 ml) granulated sugar
2 t (10 ml) finely grated lemon zest
Confectioners' sugar, for topping

Lightly butter the bottom and sides of a 9-inch (23-cm) springform pan.
Peel, core, and cut apples into ¼-inch (6-mm) thick slices.

In a large skillet over very low heat, melt the butter.
Pour most of the melted butter into a large bowl and set aside.
Add the apple slices to the remaining butter in the skillet and cook, stirring occasionally, until the apples are tender, about 10 minutes.

Remove from the heat and let cool.

Preheat oven to 375 F (190 C) degrees.

In another bowl, stir together the flour, baking powder, and salt.
In the large bowl with the melted butter, whisk in the eggs until well blended.
Add the vanilla, brandy, sugar, and lemon zest.
Pour the wet ingredients into the bowl with the flour mixture and stir until well combined.

Pour apples into the springform pan and spoon the batter on top of the apples, smoothing the top.

Place springform pan on a baking sheet and bake until the cake is lightly browned, about 40 minutes.
Run a knife around the edge of the pan, and let the cake cool in the pan to set.
When cool, remove rim and place the cake on a serving plate.

Just before serving, dust with confectioners' sugar and add a scoop of vanilla gelato or vanilla ice cream to each portion, if desired.

Serves 6 to 8

Rustic Cherry Torta
Torta Rustica di Ciliegie

Cherries are perfect with this cake, but you can use other fruit such as blackberries, strawberries, or blueberries. Crème fraîche is not an Italian staple—you could use heavy cream in its place. Sometimes it is hard to find crème fraîche in the supermarket and it can be quite expensive. I've included a recipe to make your own crème fraîche, which is very easy but needs to be done about three days ahead.

Pastry
1 cup (250 ml) pastry or all-purpose flour
3 T (45 ml) granulated sugar
½ t (2 ml) salt
6 T (90 ml) cold unsalted butter (¾ stick), cut into pieces
1 large egg yolk

Put the flour, sugar, and salt in a food processor fitted with the steel blade. Add the butter pieces and pulse until the mixture forms pea-size pieces. Add egg yolk and pulse until dough comes together. Do not overmix.

Transfer dough onto a large piece of plastic wrap and wrap up, flattening and forming the dough into a disc. Refrigerate at least one hour before rolling out.

Preheat oven to 400 F (200 C) degrees.

On a lightly floured surface, roll dough into a circle about 3 inches (7.5 cm) larger than the bottom surface of a 9-inch (23-cm) springform pan.
Press into the bottom of the pan and up the sides about 2 inches (5 cm).
Trim the edges of the dough with a table knife to make it even. Crust will be higher than the filling.
Place parchment with dried beans or pie weights on top of crust.
Bake for 15 minutes, carefully remove parchment and weights and bake another 5 minutes.

Turn oven temperature down to 350 F (190 C) degrees.

Filling
2 cups (500 ml) cherries, pitted and cut in half
2 eggs
½ cup (125 ml) granulated sugar
1 cup (250 ml) crème fraîche
½ t (2 ml) pure vanilla extract

Arrange cherries, rounded side up, on the bottom of the crust.
Beat the eggs with the sugar. Stir in the crème fraîche and vanilla extract.
Pour the custard over the cherries and bake until set, about 30 to 40 minutes.

Serves 6 to 8

Homemade Crème Fraîche
2 cups (500 ml) heavy whipping cream (pasteurized, not ultra-pasteurized or sterilized)
½ cup (125 ml) buttermilk

Pour the cream and buttermilk into a large sterile glass canning jar.
Screw on the top and let sit on your counter for 12 to 24 hours, or until thickened.
Stir and refrigerate for 2 days before using.

Tiramisu

Tiramisu is a classic Italian dessert made with espresso, mascarpone cheese, whipped cream, ladyfingers (*Savoiardi*), and a custard called *zabaglione*, pronounced "zah bahl YOH nay." Tiramisu roughly translated means "pick me up" or "lift me up." It is best if you make it early the morning before you serve it and refrigerate it at least 8 hours. Traditionally it is layered in a rectangular baking dish. I like to layer it in a small (7 ½-inch/18-cm) round springform pan with the ladyfingers lining the sides, very much like a Charlotte cake. If you use this size pan, you will have extra ladyfingers and zabaglione.

Zabaglione
4 large egg yolks
½ cup (100 g) granulated sugar
3 T (45 ml) Marsala wine
Pinch of salt

Using a hand-held mixer on low speed, beat the egg yolks and sugar in a heatproof bowl set over a saucepan of barely simmering water until the mixture is thick and creamy, about 5 minutes.
Do not let the bottom of the bowl touch the simmering water or it will cook the eggs. You just want to kill any bacteria that may be in the raw egg yolks.
Add the Marsala and salt and beat a few more seconds. Cover and refrigerate until cool.

Espresso Syrup
1 cup (250 ml) brewed espresso, or 2 T instant espresso dissolved in 1 cup (250 ml) water
1 t (5 ml) granulated sugar
1 cup (250 ml) boiling water
2 T (30 ml) Marsala wine

While the custard is cooling in the refrigerator, pour the espresso into a medium-size bowl and add the sugar to dissolve. Let cool, stir in the Marsala, and set aside.

Filling
1 (8 oz/250 g) container mascarpone cheese (1 cup)
1 cup (250 ml) heavy whipping cream
¼ cup (60 ml) granulated sugar
18 to 36 Italian ladyfingers (Savoiardi)
Unsweetened cocoa powder
Dark and white chocolate shavings, for garnish

Place the mascarpone into a large bowl and set aside to warm slightly.

In another bowl, using a hand-held mixer, beat the whipping cream and sugar until soft peaks form.
Fold the whipped cream into the mascarpone.
Fold in the chilled zabaglione and whisk gently to remove any big lumps. Cover and refrigerate.

Use a 9-inch (23-cm) square glass pan to make a smaller dessert or a larger rectangular glass pan. Or you can use a round springform pan, as shown.

Working with one at a time, quickly dip the ladyfingers into the bowl with the espresso mixture. Place the ladyfingers in the bottom of the pan to make a layer.

If using a round pan, cut the ladyfingers in half to shorten and fit upright around the edge of the pan. Do not dip these into the espresso.
Cut more ladyfingers to fit into the bottom of the pan, then dip those in espresso and place them into the bottom of the pan to make a layer.

Spread one third of the custard over.
Repeat with another layer of ladyfingers, dipped in espresso.
Spread with custard and repeat with the remaining ladyfingers and a final layer of custard.
Cover and refrigerate 8 to 10 hours.

Remove ring from pan, sprinkle with cocoa powder and decorate with chocolate shavings.
Serve chilled.

Serves 6 to 8

Molten Chocolate Espresso Cakes
Tortino al Cioccolato con Crema al Caffè

Isn't it incredible that dark chocolate, butter, sugar, and eggs always makes the most delicious dessert? Indulge once in a while!

Softened butter
1 T (15 ml) granulated sugar

6 oz (30 g) fine-quality semisweet chocolate (preferably 70% cacao), finely chopped
½ cup (125 ml) unsalted butter (1 stick)
A pinch of salt
16 oz (500 ml) heavy whipping cream (1 pint), divided
2 t (10 ml) espresso powder
1 t (5 ml) pure vanilla extract
⅓ cup (75 ml) granulated sugar
2 large eggs
2 large egg yolks
½ cup (125 ml) all-purpose flour

Butter and sugar 6 (6 oz/185 g) ramekins, place on a baking tray, and set aside.

In a heavy saucepan, heat chocolate, butter, salt, and ¼ cup (60 ml) of the cream over low heat, whisking until chocolate has melted and mixture is smooth.
Remove from heat and whisk in the espresso powder and vanilla.

In a medium bowl, beat the sugar with the eggs and yolks at high speed, until thick and light in color, for about 5 minutes. Beat in the flour for another minute.
Fold egg mixture, one third at a time, into the chocolate mixture until blended.

Divide batter evenly between ramekins. You can make these ahead by wrapping well and refrigerating up to 24 hours. Let come to room temperature before baking.

Pour the rest of the heavy whipping cream into a bowl and beat until soft peaks form. Cover and chill until ready to serve.

Preheat oven to 400 F (200 C) degrees.

Place ramekins on a baking sheet and bake until edges are set but centers still jiggle, about 8 to 10 minutes.

Cool for about 3 minutes, then run a table knife around the sides of the cups to loosen the cakes and invert onto plates.
Dust with confectioners' sugar and serve immediately with a dollop of whipped cream, lightly sweetened with sugar.

Serves 6

Casa Cannoli

Just between you and me, I don't make my own cannoli shells. You can find them in Italian grocery stores and typically they come in boxes of 6 large or 12 mini cannoli. Cannoli began as a Sicilian pastry dessert that originated in the Palermo area and were traditionally prepared as a treat during Carnevale. I had the most delicious ones in Positano and Amalfi in Italy. They were prepared with the inside of the shell coated with dark chocolate . . . *delizioso*!

1 ½ cups (375 ml) cold water
½ cup (125 ml) plus 2 T (30 ml) confectioners' sugar
1 lb (500 g) whole milk ricotta cheese
¼ t (1 ml) ground cinnamon
¼ cup (60 ml) mini semisweet chocolate chips (very important to use mini chips)

6 large cannoli shells
Melted semisweet chocolate for coating shells (optional)
Toasted unsalted pistachio nuts or halved Maraschino cherries for garnish
Confectioners' sugar, for dusting

In a heavy saucepan, slowly simmer the water with the confectioners' sugar for about 30 minutes until it becomes a heavy syrup and has reduced to about ½ cup (125 ml). Let cool.

Place the ricotta cheese in a bowl, drizzle the syrup over it and add the cinnamon. Mix together, cover bowl and place in the refrigerator for about one hour.

Remove bowl and put the ricotta mixture into a fine mesh strainer. Suspend the strainer over the same bowl, cover, and return to refrigerator for another hour or two.

Coat the inside of each shell with melted chocolate, if preferred, and let harden.

Remove the ricotta cheese from the refrigerator and press the mixture through a ricer into a bowl (you can also use a food mill using the smallest disk). Stir in the chocolate chips.
Using a pastry bag fitted with a ¾-inch (18-mm) star tip, pipe the filling into each shell.
You may also use a small spoon to do this.

Dust with confectioners' sugar, then decorate the ends with the pistachio nuts or cherry halves.

Serves 6

Acknowledgements

First of all, I want to thank my husband, Robert Casazza, for designing the book, the book cover, drawings, all of the recipe pages, and the layouts of our old family photos.

I want to thank my son Brandon Casazza, a professional photographer, for his expert advice on lighting and camera settings.

I want to thank my preliminary proofreaders who are my family members:
Angie Casazza (my daughter)
Dotti Vallone (my sister)
Cindy Casazza (my daughter-in-law)
Rose Casazza (my sister-in-law)
Ann Nelson (my cousin by marriage)

I want to thank my preliminary proofreaders who are the best friends—ever:
Federica Montagna (Positano, Italy)
Lello Porzio (Positano, Italy)
Joan Schaumberg (Washington, D.C. & Santa Barbara, California)
Diana Rich, PhD (Washington, D.C.)
Sharon Kaminski (Seattle, Washington)
Pam Fry (Salt Spring Island, Canada & Palm Springs, California)
Gail Neylan (Alexandria, Virginia & Bethany Beach, Delaware)
Catherine Roberti (Seattle, Washington)
Barb Wellman (Houston, Texas & Victoria, Canada)
John Wellman, MD (Houston, Texas & Victoria, Canada)
Amy Carlson (Seattle, Washington & Guemes Island, Washington)
Vivian de Visser (Dadeville, Alabama)
Lauri Basso Langton (Seattle, Washington)

I also want to thank our family members for sharing some of their old family photos:
Christopher Casazza (New Windsor, Maryland)
Neil Novello (Boston, Massachusetts)
Vince Novello (Tampa, Florida)
Vince Greco (Portsmouth, Virginia)
Tina Bachas (Richmond, Virginia)
Fred Brown III (Richmond, Virginia)

Finally I want to thank my editor and proofreader, Lisa Gordanier, of Hidden Hand Editing.

General Recipe Index

PASTA & GNOCCHI, continued

PIZZA & FOCACCIA

PORK (Maiale)

SALADS (Insalate)

SALADS (Insalate), continued

SEAFOOD (Frutti di Mare)

SIDE DISHES (Contorni)

SOUPS (Zuppe)

Recipes 30 Minutes and Under

A Few Words About Lee Casazza

Born and raised on Capitol Hill in Washington, D.C., Lee Casazza is a genuine "foodie" who loves to cook. Her interest in cooking started with her family's southern background; growing up, her favorite place to be was in the kitchen helping her mom prepare their many southern-style recipes.

In 1967, Lee married Robert Paul Casazza, and her love of Italian cooking began. Bob and Lee would often drive to Richmond, Virginia, for Sunday dinners at the home of his grandparents, Ernest and Elisabeth Novello. This spot was a favorite destination for the extended family, with as many as twenty relatives, attending. Sunday gravy and homemade pastas were prepared by Elisabeth, affectionately known as "Mamaw." It was where the entire family experienced "Old World" and "New World" recipes developed over many years, helping to define what Italian-American cooking has become today.

Lee is the fortunate recipient of recipes and secrets shared by both Mamaw and Bob's mother Marie, who both had a firsthand knowledge of all the recipes passed down by generations of the Casazza and Noviello families. Over the years, Italian food has become an important part of Lee's life. New cookbooks, articles, famous chefs, restaurants, and travels to Italy have been constant inspirations. These exposures to the world of Italian food preparation have allowed her to develop her own unique techniques.

In Washington, D.C., Lee had a successful career in real estate. After the family moved to Seattle in 1994, she was ready for new challenges. Lee designed and built a home and cottage on an island in the Pacific Northwest; she was both a carpenter and the general contractor on the projects. Today, Lee is an avid volunteer genealogist and an active member of the Daughters of the American Revolution.

Lee created "Big Mamma's Italian-American Cooking" blog in March of 2011. This blog has developed into an ongoing collection of recipes passed down by the Casazza and Noviello families, with frequent new additions from Lee. It also includes historical family photos, recipe origins, and helpful preparation tips. Her blog has attracted followers from countries around the world.

As the author, chef, photographer, and researcher, Lee has put her "Italian heart" into this cookbook. Her love for her Italian-American family and her culinary devotion to Italian-American cooking has combined to produce the most delicious collection of recipes you'll ever find.
What truly sets this cookbook apart are the talents of the four ladies in this Italian-America family. Meet Teresa Lapetina Greco, "Big Mamma," Elisabeth Greco Noviello, "Mamaw," Marie Noviello Casazza, and Lee Casazza.

Buon appetito!

238